Education Skewed

Education Skewed

A Closer Look at the Educating of the Minority

Joyce Thomas, Ed.D

Copyright © 2009 by Joyce Thomas, Ed.D.

Library of Congress Control Number: 2009909730
ISBN: Hardcover 978-1-4415-8129-7
Softcover 978-1-4415-8128-0

All rights reserved. No part of this book may be reproduced or transmitted in any form or by any means, electronic or mechanical, including photocopying, recording, or by any information storage and retrieval system, without permission in writing from the copyright owner.

This book was printed in the United States of America.

To order additional copies of this book, contact:
Xlibris Corporation
1-888-795-4274
www.Xlibris.com
Orders@Xlibris.com
60251

CONTENTS

Preface ix

Chapter 1:   Introduction 1

    1. Evolution of Special Education
    2. Purpose

Chapter 2:   Pledge to the Specials 5

    1. Federal
    2. New York State
        a. Deinstitutionalization
    3. Resiliency

Chapter 3:   Revolution of Special Education 18

    A. Placement
        1. Testing
        2. Minorities
        3. Mainstreaming
        4. Inclusion
    B. Conflicts/Implementation
        1. Eleven Different Districts
        2. Profile of Eleven (A-K) School Districts in New York
            — Tables 1, 2, 3, 4, and 5
            — Figures 1 and 2
        3. Socioeconomics

Chapter 4:   Masks Unveiled 42

    1. Funding
    2. Resources
    3. Politics

       4. Accountability

Chapter 5:   Focus on Success 51

    A. Support Data
        1. Learning Style
        2. IEP
        3. Social Interaction
        4. Build Strength
        5. Self-esteem and Character Development
        6. Stable Environment
        7. Freedom of Choice
        8. Unique Needs and Instruction
    B. Case Studies
        1. 1-5
        2. Discussion

Chapter 6:   Anecdotal Studies 67

    A. Observation and Interviews
        1. Five Different Schools
        2. Discussion

Chapter 7:   Ineffective Strategies 74

    A. State Mandates
        1. Pressure on Schools
    B. Attitude Toward Special Education
        1. Community/State
        2. Administration
        3. Teacher/School
        4. Dropout
    C. SURR

Chapter 8:   NCLB's Contradictory Message 82

    A. Left Behind
        1. African Americans
        2. Disadvantaged/Poor/Women
        3. Medication/Substance Abusers

    B. Examination Faux Pas
        1. Constraints
        2. Push Up to Push Out

Chapter 9: Unprepared for Independence 91

    A. Blatant Disparities
    B. Past Graduates 1995-2003
        1. Data/Survey
        2. Figure 3
        3. Discussion
    C. Executive Changes 94
        1. Minorities—Underserved

Chapter 10: Complementary Study 97

    A. Data Collection & Analysis 98
        1. Figures 4 and 5
        2. Tables 6, 7, 8, and 9
        3. Discussion and Assumption
    B. Graduation 2008 102

Chapter 11: Summation 103

    1. Discussion and Conclusion 103
    2. Implication 105
    3. Recommendations: 107

Abbreviations 109

Glossary 111

References 117

Index 127

Preface

The ratification of the Fourteenth Amendment has allowed for equal education for all. Yet blacks (Negroes / African Americans) are consistently denied the right as evidenced in *Plessy v. Ferguson* in 1896, *Brown v. Board of Education* in 1954, *Arkansas 9* in 1957, and *Parents Involved in Community Schools v. Seattle School District No. 7* in 2007.

It has been a constant battle to equally, appropriately, and effectively educate black minority students. Unfortunately, many of these students are confined in economic poverty and social destruction. They are undereducated, maladjusted, misguided, miseducated, misjudged, and jobless without marketable skills or self-motivation to obtain access to a productive life. They are passed over, earmarked for failure, and left in the throes of abuse, isolation, and self-destruction. Too often, parents and guardians are silenced by the powerful legal barriers put up by the education process, thereby leaving these children devoid of effective education and the sound foundation for success in life.

Furthermore, it is evident that a disproportionate number of minority students are identified and labeled as special children or children with disabilities. This shows a strong correlation to hiding, segregating, isolating, and subjugating to black students, paving the way of an entrapped, continuous cycle of failure, rejection, and criminal behavior.

Although the federal laws and state mandates stipulate that students with disabilities be educated in a "least restrictive environment" to receive their highest potential, these children are herded to schools with limited service providers, little resources, less qualified teachers, and/or teachers who are less enthused to teach them. As a result, the unique needs of these newly discovered minority special education students are seldom addressed, leaving them unfulfilled, frustrated, inadequate, and hopeless, confirming the myth that they are inferior and incapable of learning.

The intent of this research is to highlight some of the factors that affect these minority special education students, take away the mask that veils the alienation and inadequacy of assessment, the ineffective inappropriate intervention and implementation of services, and to examine the validity and purpose of the mandatory standardized tests and exit examinations that determine the future of these students.

With the odds against them, these students are further humiliated by the exit strategies imposed upon them to fulfill the mandates of NCLB. Too often, districts are required to comply with the new state mandates that they are forced to provide testing accommodations to students who are inadequately prepared. Such accommodations include tests read, clarified, explained, written for, and much more. The accommodations only help to correct superficial inequities, leaving ingrained deep within the societal factors that indulge them to incurable malignancy of the mind.

Losing their ability to choose or to think creatively, the students are guaranteed a bright future. With the glimmer of hope looming, they are then led like patients strapped on a gurney ready for open-heart surgery, relying solely on the word of the medical staff that everything would be fine. The students then proceed to sit for these intimidating examinations for which they are unprepared. In some instances, they are prompted to pass—which they do, boosting their self-esteem as well as the percentage of passes on the SED report card for the respective school district.

Like surviving the surgery, similarly the students get through the examinations somewhat hopeful to enter higher academia or the job market. Their self-esteem and glimmer of hope are quickly dashed when both organizations test them for eligibility and acceptability. Interestingly, the employer and the higher education authority are expected to create a "least restrictive environment" similar to what the students were guaranteed. Eventually, the students are rejected because they are not even minimally prepared, leaving one to ponder on the following:

- How prepared for a job or higher education are these students?
- Who is to blame?
- Did the education process fail them?
- What factors contribute to their failure?
- What message did this experience send?
- Are the minority students better served if they are labeled as special education students?
- Rather, is "special education" a way of further subjugation of the black race?

No one should be surprised if these students drop out before the exit examinations that left their senior comrades stigmatized, humiliated, worthless, and stripped of their dignity and respect.

Therefore, it behooves administrators, teachers, parents, and the community to work together for the common good of every child in the district. Moreover, race, ethnicity, income, or cultural background should enhance, not diminish, the extent of education meted to minority, or in fact, all students.

As well, there is a need to advocate for well-trained, dedicated educators who—as skilled mechanics repair the broken spokes and the flat tires, making the vehicle new again and the envy of all—are sensitive to the diverse needs of each child regardless of race. And like that mechanic, those dedicated educators must help prepare the students for empowerment, employment, self-sufficiency, and productive citizenry.

1

INTRODUCTION

Although the amendment to the constitution stipulates "equal education for all," civil rights advocates have been trying continuously to enforce the same for minority students. In fact, a disproportionate number of these students have been classified or placed in special education classes where they can be accommodated well enough to achieve their maximum potential. Yet studies after studies show that they are failing miserably nationwide, further widening the gap that the NCLB (2001) intended to close. Consequently, these minorities end up undereducated, miseducated, frustrated, left out, and burdened heavily with many wavering thoughts and speculations, giving rise to one basic, troubling question, is special education helping or hurting minority students?

The originator of this research has decided to answer that question and more through research, observation, and surveys in New York and the use of the following words and phrases interchangeably:

- Special education
- Special needs
- Disabled children
- Special children
- Developmentally disabled persons
- Mentally ill
- Exceptional children
- Individuals with disabilities

Educating special-needs children requires trained and skilled educators jointly with adequate funding. One would question, why the extra effort to support these special children, or why does special education demand such delicate handling? Notably, for more than seven decades, advocates, organizations, parents, educators, policy makers, and researchers have been continuously devising methods to intervene, normalize, and treat special-needs children who were impaired physically, psychologically, mentally, and/or developmentally delayed. Every effort was to enable special children to become productive, self-sufficient, and independent. Even today, the venture is so challenging that the federal and state governments spend much time and money, consistently changing and upgrading laws, beginning with PL 94-142 in 1975 to No Child Left Behind (NCLB) in 2001. The intent then and now is to give special-needs children a fair chance in life consistent with the Fourteenth Amendment.

However, there are concerns as to whether these children are receiving equal, effective, and appropriate intervention and treatment. This persistent action is crucial because special-needs children span decades as a society under adversity in which there were little or no options available to them.

Evolution of Special Education

In the early twentieth century, people with special needs received services in large public institutions, or their families cared for them with little financial help from the government (Davis et. al. 2005). This was a great improvement from earlier centuries when America and other parts of the world did not tolerate any special-needs or disabled children. At that time, they suffered all types of abuses and were condemned as incapable of improvement or simply forgotten. Then the French began to advocate help for the weak and disabled in the 1700s (Including the Disabled Student, n.d.).

By the turn of the twentieth century, compulsory education and child labor laws, as well as huge numbers of European immigrants, forced American public schools to enroll a significant number of special-needs children, resulting in the creation of special education classes. In the 1920s, special education classes became established, complete with its own curriculum and teachers, and recognized nationwide. In spite of the establishment of special education classes, parents were concerned with segregation of the classes. Then in 1975, some of them challenged the delivery of service in isolation. This propelled the movement from institutionalization to mainstreaming and inclusion of special-needs children into regular classrooms (Including the Disabled Students, n.d).

A debate of bioethics issues concluded that normalizing and deinstitutionalization did not guarantee equity for the students. Similarly, disability seemed to be shortening their life span, where abuse, misuse, and discrimination created additional factors impeding their health and development. As the bioethics issues showed, there were gross misrepresentations among poor people where over 60% of them lived below the poverty level. Besides, education, the key to empowerment, is being denied to the most disabled, leaving 67% of the disabled between the ages fifteen and sixty-four years old unemployed.

Purpose

The information piqued a deeper interest in the researcher to explore more thoroughly the situation of special-needs children, how well they are being acknowledged and served to self-sufficiency, and to explore the justification and/or correlation in classifying the minority students as special education students. As explained in the bioethics issues, updated technology, science, and medicine in the twenty-first century have not prevented disabilities or created effective ways to overcome the same. As a result, parents and educators face the daily challenge of dealing with contradictory mandates in the servicing, caring, and rehabilitating of special children. In this article, the researcher is attempting to uncover some variables that can impede or help place children in the right vehicle toward self-sufficiency and independence.

After drawing the public's attention to the plight of special-needs children, the law and advocates agreed, as depicted, that great care was essential in their education. However, with the new dimension—the poor and its fringes—added, educators realized that the job of successfully educating them became more challenging. Their effective education, therefore, would depend on the proper vehicle equipped with appropriate resources, tools, and well-trained mechanics as the first effective step, traveling along the winding and tiresome education journey garnished with intricate labyrinth of lingering questions such as follows:

- Why is the educational process failing so many black students?
- Why is there so much time, money, and effort spent on special-needs children, with little success?
- What is the psychological or emotional impact on minority students classified as special education students?

- Why do so many classified special education children drop out and disappear from the empowerment and employment radar?
- Can the educational process guarantee that all children realize the purpose of the No Child Left Behind Act?
- Are minority—particularly black—students equally served?
- Is there a double standard in the education of minority students?
- How can educators assure or prove that minority students are not burdensome to the American taxpayers but that they are employable?
- Why is there a disproportionate number of minority students classified as special education students?
- Is the focus in school districts more geared to securing a good test score rather than a sound and lasting education?
- What is more beneficial or adaptable today, *Brown v. Board of Education* or *Plessy v. Ferguson?*
- Why is a successful black person who luckily escaped the special education classification recognized as the "First This or First That"? Does this motivate a young black person?
- How do employers view black employees?
- Who is mostly to blame for the significant number of incarcerations of blacks?
- Who is responsible for the dysfunction of these children and later adults?
- Are researchers overlooking the simple variables that may and can make a difference in effectively educating or treating these children?

In this paper, the researcher intends to identify successes and failures, compare variables, and identify other variable(s) in the ongoing effort to bring special education children close to empowerment, employment, and self-sufficiency and to point out the assimilation of special education students with minority students.

2

PLEDGE TO THE SPECIALS

The movement away from institutionalization of special children made the public worldwide aware of the existence of the disabled as people. Under the Charter of the United Nations and the International Bill of Human Rights, disabled persons are entitled to exercise all the civil, political, economic, social, and cultural rights on an equal basis with other persons because they are born free and equal in dignity (Enable Human Rights an Disabled Persons, n.d.).

In the 1960s, advocates pushed for a federal role by providing leadership and funding in an effort to provide a free appropriate public education (FAPE) to children with disabilities. In 1966, Congress went a little further by establishing the Bureau of the Handicapped under Title VI of the Elementary and Secondary Education Act (ESEA). This gave rise to a number of pioneers and earmarked small amounts of federal funds for serving children with disabilities. As these programs progressed rapidly, the bureau recommended that they should merge into a single law, PL 91-230, passed in 1970 (Background and History, n.d.).

FEDERAL

Accordingly, significant court cases gave more momentum to the special needs cause. Starting with the case of *Robinson v. California* in 1962, the court ruled that the state violated the Eight Amendment by subjecting Robinson to cruel and unusual punishment in incarcerating him without rehabilitation (Incarceration without rehabilitation in significant court cases, n.d.).

Ten years later, the following court cases gave the public more insight into problems that people with disabilities faced in institutions (Law and Persons with Disabilities, n.d.).

A class action suit in Alabama, *Wyatt v. Stickney*, showed the participants' constitutional rights were violated under the Fourteenth Amendment. It was the first time that mentally retarded persons were recognized as citizens with rights.

Burham v. Georgia contradicted *Wyatt v. Stickney*. The court found that individuals in institutions had a moral right to treatment, but the state was not legally responsible to provide the treatment.

In *Jackson v. Indiana,* Jackson, who was deaf and mentally retarded, committed a crime. He was incarcerated in a mental institution with no rehabilitation for three and a half years. He was incompetent to stand trial, thus a violation of due process.

So too in *O'Connor v. Donaldson* in Florida. Donaldson's father committed him to an institution in 1957. At the time of commitment, Donaldson was neither harmful nor dangerous to himself or others. He received neither adequate treatment nor therapy. Consequently, he was awarded $38,000. The court found that it was illegal and ruled on the illegality of involuntarily institutionalizing a person who is not dangerous and who is able to function without institutional care.

In *Halderman v. Pennhurst*, where Halderman was confined involuntarily and received no rehabilitation, where the institution provided confinement and isolation, the court found the institution in violation of least restrictive environment, physical abuse, and lack of adequate supervision to be free from harm.

In *Youngberg v. Romero*, Youngberg's mother petitioned the institution to take her thirty-three-year-old son who could not communicate with others or take care of himself but exhibited violent behavior. After confinement, he suffered injuries inflicted by him and others. The mother filed suit. The court found that the rights of persons involuntarily committed to an institution are the same as those committed on a voluntary status (Law and Persons with Disabilities, n.d.).

Meantime, in the 1960s and the early 1970s, parents began to pursue state laws that would require local educational agencies (LEA) to offer special education services to students with disabilities for which they would provide partial funding. Although these were passed and supposedly followed by a number of states, and although provisions for some federal funding through PL 91-230 were put in place, "many children with disabilities remained un-served or under-served by public schools." Many more problems surfaced. Special-needs children were capturing the attention of the nation, prompting the enactment of more laws (Background and History, n.d.).

To further the public awareness of the plight of people with disabilities, two landmark federal court cases—*Pennsylvania Associated for Retarded Children v. Commonwealth of Pennsylvania*, 1972, and *Mills v. Board of Education of the District of Columbia*, 1972—tried to appease the people and curb the growing problems. The court decisions outlined that "the responsibility of states and local school districts to educate individuals with disabilities was derived from the equal protection clause of the Fourteenth Amendment of the United States Constitution." States began then to look to the federal government for more cohesion (Background and History, n.d.).

Simultaneously, in 1972, Geraldo Rivera, a reporter for television station WABC, conducted a series of investigations at Willowbrook in New York and uncovered many despicable conditions. He found overcrowding, inadequate sanitary facilities and physical and sexual abuse of residents by staff members. This resulted in a class action lawsuit filed against New York State and the federal government on March 17, 1972. A settlement in the case in 1972 mandated reforms that were not implemented immediately. However, the publicity generated the passage of numerous laws including the consent decree in following years (Science Daily: Willowbrook State School, n.d.).

New York State

The consent decree stipulated numerous laws that Governor Carey signed in 1975. The decree provided for the right to treatment, reduction in numbers of residents, and provision of normal living environment. The class for the residents provided an opportunity for growth and development in the least restrictive environment. Each class member had an individual development plan describing capabilities, needs, and services to be provided. An interdisciplinary team prepared the plan, reviewed it quarterly, and reevaluated it annually, while one member supervised and implemented it continuously. Moreover, parents and caretakers received information on all aspects of their children's activities and progress on a quarterly basis. They also assisted in the preparation and reevaluation of the development plan. In addition, all class members received a full and suitable education program or, for those over twenty-one years, at least six hours of appropriate formal daily programming (Willowbrook Consent Decree, n.d.).

In the consent decree were included rights for developmentally disabled persons in the Assistance and Bill of Rights Act with reference to the following:

Persons with developmental disabilities have a right to appropriate treatment, service and habilitation for such disabilities:

- Persons with developmental disabilities have a right to appropriate treatment service and habilitation for such disabilities,
- The treatment service and habilitation for a person with development disabilities should be designed to maximize the developmental potential of the person and should be provided in the setting that is least restrictive of the person's personal liberty;
- The Federal Government and the State both have an obligation to assure that public funds are not provided to any institution or other residential program for the disabled that does not provide appropriate treatment, services and rehabilitation or provide nourishing, well-balanced diet daily or does not provide appropriate and sufficient medical and dental services. Recipients of funds should prohibit physical restraint, excessive chemical restraint and permit visits by close relatives at reasonable hours without prior notice, and should comply with adequate fire and safety standards;
- All programs should meet standards which are designed to assure the most favorable outcomes for those served. (Willowbrook Consent Decree, n.d.)

As Haller (1999) explained, the law was clearly on the side of the parents and advocates. Public Law 94-142, the Education for All Handicapped Children Act, mandated that all school-age children with disabilities receive a free appropriate education in the least restrictive environment (LRE). It also stipulated that schools provide the children with needed special education and related services. Related services included transportation, physical therapy (PT), occupational therapy (OT), adapted physical education, and psychological assessments. "Appropriate education in the least restrictive environment" meant that children with disabilities be educated, to the maximum extent appropriate, together with children who had no disabilities. In addition, special classes, separate schooling, or other removal of children with disabilities from the regular educational environment should occur only when the nature and severity of the disability is such that education in regular classes could not be achieved satisfactorily. Before this law, many students were missing the opportunity to learn in the public institutions because of their disabilities. The public system totally excluded over one million of these children (PL 94-142 IDEA 2005).

Deinstitutionalization

The public awareness and the courts' decisions increased the deinstitutionalization of people with disabilities into public schools. As more disabled students attended regular schools, educators became concerned about the process of teaching them (Including the Disabled Student, n.d.).

Deinstitutionalization became the new approach for treating people with disabilities who, for many years, had two choices. For the affluent, there was psychotherapy; and for the others, there was the state mental hospital, with a reputation for treating patients badly. The new way of treatment gained favor in the 1950s when psychiatrists believed that the mentally ill would do better as outpatients living close to relatives and jobs. States then transferred patients from state mental hospitals to community health centers, nursing homes, and other facilities. As a result, outpatient facilities grew tremendously (Deinstitutionalization, n.d.).

Many states adopted the new approach that drastically reduced the cost of institutionalizing patients from $94,348 for institution care as opposed to $14,902 for community-based care. However, a large number of these people were only developmentally disabled. Many experts agreed that most of the people in the state hospital lived in the community if they required appropriate services (Davis et al. 2005). They also found that delivery of service, variation of rates for funding community-based services, social and political issues, and choice of setting were becoming controversial.

Some researchers reported that deinstitutionalization posed more problems. They claimed that thousands of mentally ill and developmentally disabled people eked out a pitiful existence on city streets, underground in subway tunnels, or in prisons because of misguided efforts of civil rights advocates to keep the severely ill out of hospital and treatment. Regrettably, the disabled committed almost 1,000 homicides per year, 200,000 were homeless, 28 percent foraged for food in garbage cans, and about 170,000 were in jail, costing the American taxpayers $8.5 billion per year (Torrey and Zdanowicz, n.d.; Steely, n.d.).

Other researchers claimed that deinstitutionalization did not fulfill the promise to reinvest saved money in community mental health care. Apart from that, they cautioned that the mentally disabled people who needed help the most were driven away when forced into treatment (Wieselthier and Allen 2005). Other problems surfaced because of lost jobs, which resulted in the reduction of the number of patients and the quality of patient care (Deinstitutionalization, n.d.).

Barriers to deinstitutionalize—including some families, clients, and advocacy groups—advocated for better institutional care instead of institution closures. The fact remained that the residents required treatment. Then, too, some states had inadequate medical services and lack of formal training for physicians and caregivers (Davis et al. 2005).

The authorities faced many problems in the process of implementation of the new approach. So the federal government opted to support high-quality, intensive, and professional development for all people who worked with such children to meet developmental goals to

- assist the states in funding these programs;
- encourage the growth of diversity, especially with the risk of the nation's minorities that do not speak English; and
- provide more technology services to assist in education of diverse students.

That meant that the following impairments of special-needs people be included for treatment in a regular setting:

— Specific learning disabilities
— Speech or language impairments
— Emotional disturbance
— Autism
— Mental retardation, including severe and multiple disabilities
— Orthopedic impairments
— Hearing impairments, including deafness
— Traumatic brain injury
— Visual impairment, including blindness
— Other health impairments

According to the report, these children attended schools in or near their neighborhood to help make their lives and the lives of the families who loved them much better (PL 94-142 IDEA 2005).

Resiliency

Families played an important role in life events affecting them. They bounced back and adapted to changes in the family structure or fell prey to the situation and deteriorated. For family resiliency, two main factors helped the family to cope: (1) adjustment, which involved the protection in facilitating the family in its efforts to maintain its integrity, functioning, and fulfilling developmental tasks in the face of risk factors; and (2) adaptation, which involved the function of recovery factors in promoting the family's ability to "bounce back" and adapt in family crisis.

Factors that helped a family build resiliency to adjust and adapt were problem-solving, communications, equality, spirituality, flexibility, truthfulness, hope, family hardiness, family time and routine, social support, and health. Caring for a person with disability was effective when the family showed commitment and put forth great effort to sustain family practices and routines. This maintained the family's stability and continuity in the face of adversity (McCubbin et al. 1997). They also emphasized that families used the factors that yielded the best result for the nature of the crisis.

Therefore, in the event of deinstitutionalization, parents demanded better treatment in the institution or accepted them without patient services. Negative or positive factors determined the outcome of effective resiliency. Genetics, personality, physical health, immediate family, social/peer, neighborhood/community/school, and the individual's interaction with the environment were neutral factors that generated a positive outcome. When these factors were negative, then it was harder to become resilient (Risk and Resiliency Factors 2005).

McCubbin et al. (1997) conducted extensive longitudinal research to identify the factors that appeared to play a critical role in promoting the family's ability to maintain its established patterns of functioning after challenging risk factors and fostering the family's ability to recover or bounce back quickly from misfortune and family crisis.

Some of the challenges for the participants included experiences in death, broken families, empty nest, retirement, interracial couples, children left alone for long periods of time, teenage pregnancy, military members held captive or missing in action, sickness, and other family tragedies.

As background for their research, the researchers cited numerous works done by the following: Werner (1984); Werner and Smith (1982); Garmezy (1991a, 1991b); Luthar (1987); Rutter (1990); Garmezy (1987); Garmezy and Masten (1991); Luthar and Zigler (1992); Luthar (1991); and Luthar, Doernberger, and Zigler (1993). McCubbin et al. (1997) concluded that families used the following natural critical resource factors to recover from challenges:

- Family integration
- Family support and esteem building

- Family recreation orientation, control, and organization
- Family optimism and mastery

Added information from research indicated that families, especially the parent(s), were paramount to the effective rehabilitation of special-needs people. Rod Paige, former U.S. secretary of education, agreed with the information by saying, "There are no more powerful advocates for children than a parent armed with information and options" (Tools for Student Success 2005).

PL 94-142 mandated that children be educated in a "least restrictive environment" with free and appropriate education. Such a learning institute could be a regular school where educators or teachers implemented the requirement. Implementing the policy included coordinating with other educational service agencies, practicing nondiscriminatory testing as well as creating an individual education plan (IEP). They also monitored current educational objectives and means of implementation. It gave the parents or guardian the right to participate in the planning and implementation of educational or rehabilitative services to their children with disabilities (PL 94-142 IDEA 2005).

The public law requires that after a referral by a teacher, a pre-assessment is held between the parent or guardian and the special education coordinator. Following the pre-assessment, the parent or guardian must consent in writing before an evaluation can begin. A team of professionals evaluates the child and looks for specific strengths and weaknesses to determine if there is a need for special education services after which they assess the child in the area of the suspected disability. At that juncture, the parent has the prerogative to ask that other areas be assessed. The tests administered must be objective and in the child's native language. This evaluation is a team process, including the parent, thereby eliminating one single opinion or evaluation.

Accordingly, within forty-five school days, the school evaluates the child, conducts a team meeting, and develops an appropriate educational plan. All professionals who would assess the child should be at this meeting where specified details as to strengths, weaknesses, assessments, and recommendations are discussed. If the child's case is unique, they write an IEP detailing the placement and services. Parents are encouraged to educate themselves about the laws, needs of their children, the school's policies, their options, and their rights. They should know the basic language and terms and how to find and work with the experts and professionals. They must know how to cope with their child's disability too, how to work through the maze of laws and medical terms, and how to support the child and participate at the IEP meeting. These are important tools that parents can use to build resiliency necessary to help their children (Haller 1999; Public laws regarding special education, n.d.; McCubbin et al. 1997).

Other research expressed the importance of including the parent's or guardian's financial resources in the child's education plan. This was to ensure that the disabled child had effective access to and/or received education, training, health care services, rehabilitation services, preparation for employment, and recreation opportunities in a way conducive to the child's achieving the fullest possible social integration and individual development. The plan also incorporated the child's cultural and spiritual development (Enable Human Rights and Disabled Persons, n.d.).

Helping the disabled proved to be an ongoing process, and advocates pursued more creative ways for further enhancements. To achieve this help for the disabled, PL 94-142 added many amendments. In 1978, PL 95-606, the Amateur Sports Act was added. It allowed special students to participate in amateur sports, thereby giving special-needs youngsters a feeling of recognition and inclusion. In 1981, there was another amendment, PL 97-35 Title XIX of the Social Security Act, which allowed states to apply for Medicaid funds to provide home and community-based services for children who were at risk of being institutionalized or were residing in an institution.

Some reports indicated that although parents were included in the assessment and placement procedures, many of them were not knowledgeable beyond basics. The parents needed further education and information about the process and procedures regarding disabilities and rehabilitation. So in 1983, PL 98-199 was added to the Education of the Handicapped Act, allowing federal funding to develop parent training and information centers (PIC), giving parents the opportunity to learn how to protect the rights that PL 94-142 guaranteed their child. PL 98-199 also provided financial incentives to expand services for children from birth to age three and the initiatives for transition services from school to adult living for students with disabilities (Woolfolk 1998; Public laws regarding special education, n.d.).

These acts and laws not only helped the disabled, but also opened awareness for legal issues. Congress again attached an amendment to offset legal problems. PL 99-372 Handicapped Children's Protection Act (1986) allowed reimbursements for reasonable legal loss to parents or guardian if a court ruled in their favor in a hearing or court action (Law and Exceptional Students, n.d.).

Added to that law in 1986 was PL 99-457, Education of the Handicapped Act Amendments (1986). The amendments, also known as the Early Intervention Amendments to PL 92-142, extended FAPE to all children ages three to five by October 1991 (Section 619, Part B) in all states that wanted to participate. All fifty states and even states that did not have public schools for children this age participated. In Section 619, Part H, a new program was created for infants, toddlers, and their families, which required the development of an individualized family service plan (IFSP) for each child or family served (Law and Exceptional Students, n.d.).

Even more opportunities opened up to special children. PL 100-407 Technology Related Assistance for Individuals with Disabilities Act (1988), also known as the Tech Act, recognized that students with disabilities needed special equipment to perform better and more independently. This act also authorized funding to allow states to create statewide systems of technological assistance to meet their needs. Then in the same year came PL 100-360 Medicare Catastrophic Coverage Act (1988). It allowed states to obtain limited funds for IEP-related services and for early intervention/family support services as defined in the IFSP (Public Laws regarding Special Education, n.d.).

At the end of the decade, there was yet another amendment added to PL 94-142. Public Law 101-239 Medicare Amendments (1989) expanded Medicaid's early and periodic screening, diagnosis, and treatment (EPSDT) and allowed Medicaid funds for medically necessary treatment without regard for limits of a state's Medicaid plan (Woolfolk 1998).

There was yet room for improvement and expansion of the laws. The 1990s seemed to revolutionize the alteration with five more amendments to help special children. The five amendments enacted in that year were as follows:

- In 1990, PL 101-336, the American with Disabilities Act (ADA), extended Section 504 of PL 93-112 by requiring the right of equal access and reasonable accommodation in employment and services provided by both private and public sectors.
- PL 101-392, the Carl D. Perkins Vocational and Applied Technology Education Act (1990), required that students with disabilities receive vocational education in the least restrictive environment when appropriate and be a part of the individualized education plan. This law also required that individuals with disabilities receive equal access to vocational programs (i.e., recruitment, enrollment, and placement activities).
- In 1990, PL 101-476, the Individuals with Disabilities Education Act (IDEA), also known as the Education of the Handicapped Act Amendments of 1990, renamed the earlier EHA laws and their

amendments. PL 101-476 replaced the word *handicapped* with the word *disabled* and therefore expanded the services for these students. IDEA reaffirmed PL 94-142's requirements of a free appropriate public education (FAPE) through an individualized education plan with related service and due process procedures. This act also supported the amendments to PL 94-142 that expanded the entitlement in all states to ages three to twenty-one. Designated assistive technology as a related service in IEPs strengthened the law's commitment to greater inclusion in community schools (least restrictive placement), provided funding for infant and toddler early intervention programs, and required that by age sixteen, every student would have explicitly written in the IEP a plan for transition to employment or postsecondary education.

- PL 101-496, the Developmental Disabilities Assistance and Bill of Rights Act of 2000, promoted community acceptance and inclusion for all people with developmental disabilities. It also provided funds to state protection and advocacy agencies for disabled people.
- PL 101-508, the Child Care and Development Block Grant Act (1990), a part of the Omnibus Budget Reconciliation Act (OBRA), focused on the need for child care throughout the country. It emphasized the need and encouraged the inclusion of children with "special needs" in those child care programs, which were developed by the states as a result of the funds provided to each state that submitted a comprehensive plan for child care (Woolfolk 1998).

Still these amendments and laws needed more expansion to cover more characteristics of people with disabilities. The rights of the disabled, their wishes, and their needs required protection. PL 102-569 Rehabilitation Act Amendment of 1992 revised and expanded the programs of PL 93-112. The new law, PL 102-569, included provisions that ensured consideration of the individual's wishes during the rehabilitation process, especially the writing of the individualized written rehabilitation plan (IWRP), which included a statement about participant's involvement in its development. It also defined vocational services transition and supported employment services: those who were eligible for these services, those who needed intensive supported employment services to enter or retain employment, and those with the most severe disabilities. PL 102-569 also emphasized that the basis for the number of hours provided for individuals be a maximum possible amount, based on their strengths, resources, interests, and concerns.

The individuals with disabilities received freedom to express themselves with federal and state help. When put in specific categories, they seemed to be less threatening and confusing. There were major areas of consideration (Woolfolk 1998; Law and Exceptional Students, n.d.):

- Free appropriate public education (FAPE)
- PL 94-142, Education for all Handicapped Children Act (1975)
- PL 99-457, Education of the Handicapped Act Amendments (1986)
- PL 101-476, Individuals with Disabilities Education Act (1990)
- Individualized education plan (IEP)
- PL 101-392, the Carl D. Perkins Vocational and Applied Technology Education Act (1990)
- PL 100-360, Medicare Catastrophic Coverage Act (1988)
- Least restrictive environment (LRE)
- Individualized family service plan (IFSP)
- Assistive technology
- PL 100-407, Technology-Related Assistance for Individuals with Disabilities Act (1988)
- Access and reasonable accommodation
- PL 93-112, Rehabilitation Act (1973)
- PL 101-336, Americans with Disabilities Act (1990)
- Individualized written rehabilitation program
- PL 102-569 Rehabilitation Act Amendment of 1992
- Parent information centers (PIC)
- PL 98-199, Education of the Handicapped Act Amendments (1983)

The changes became very challenging for a teacher to implement in a classroom where he or she had to coordinate with other educational service agencies, practice nondiscriminatory testing, set high standards, and create an individual education plan for each special student. This included monitoring the progress and generating educational objectives, goals, and means for implementation. The teacher also had to integrate these students and work to accommodate their needs as well as the nondisabled students in the class.

Along with the positive results on the part of the federal government to accommodate special-needs children were also ingrained the support of high-quality, intensive professional development for all people who work with such children to meet developmental goals to

- assist the states in funding these programs;

- encourage the growth of diversity, especially with the rise of the nation's minorities that do not speak English; and
- provide more technological services to assist in the education of diverse students. In so doing, the federal government made sure that all children with disabilities attended schools that were in their neighborhood capable of teaching them free of charge and ensuring they received basic skills that everyone in the United States is entitled to receive.

However, the government continued to expand the mandates for people with disabilities. Then on January 3, 2001, Congress passed another education act.

The new act intended to cover every corner, inch, path, and fill in the gaps of the past laws. The Elementary and Secondary Education Act (ESEA) was "to close the achievement gap with accountability, flexibility, and choice so that no child is left behind, now cited as the 'No Child Left Behind Act of 2001.'" The extremely broad law covered many bases including private schools, immigrants, allocation of funds, Native Americans, state grants, twenty-first-century schools, and numerous others. It not only covered special-needs children, but also every child in the United States and United States territories around the world (Elementary and Secondary Education Act, n.d.).

3

REVOLUTION OF SPECIAL EDUCATION

The laws and acts guaranteed that all children including special-needs children would have a thorough and appropriate education, enabling them to succeed in life and live independently. Isolation and deinstitutionalization began the shift toward recognizing and allowing all special-needs children to reach their maximum potential.

PLACEMENT

Identifying and treating students in a humane way added to the challenges of placement, quality programs, evaluation, accountability, and due process for the educators. Having the laws and mandates were only one small part of the whole picture of the educational process (Sametz and McLoughlin 1985; Wieselthier and Allen 1999). How to educate children with cultural diversities piled on added challenges for many school districts and administrators. As Cech (2007) denoted, assessing student for placement becomes questionable. Parents have the options to determine the race of their children. Nonetheless, any racial identification made on behalf of a student who was identified as Hispanic would not be counted in the data submitted to the federal government. Besides, a black or white student who was also identified as Hispanic would be counted only as Hispanic.

Testing

Assessment became the first step in determining and drawing up an appropriate plan for each disabled student, propelling it as testing, a very important tool in the evaluating process. Nevertheless, as some researchers observed, testing presented problems because they were not reliable. Schwarz and Burt (January 1995) demonstrated that standardized tests were normed primarily on native English speakers and younger students. Nonetheless, assessors did not use the appropriate type of testing, on people of different languages and culture. In addition, such procedures caused inappropriate testing, which in turn placed many more minority children than other children in special education classes. Inevitably, most students were referred for academic problems (Hosp and Reschly 2004).

Minorities

Hosp and Reschly (2004) also maintained that special education classes comprised of a disproportionate representation of certain minority students. In their study, they used variables from previous studies and added achievement variables to demographics and economic variables. They also expanded the race variables to include racial/ethnic groups (American Indian, Asian / Pacific Islander, and Latino) and a learning disability category. The base for their research was the report of over four decades indicating a constant and consistent pattern of disproportionality documented and demonstrated to be robust and steady over time. They used data gathered from three sources.

The first source was the Elementary and Secondary Schools Civil Rights Compliance Report (OCR data set; U.S. Department of Education 2000). Twenty-five variables were coded—the number of students from each of the five federal race/ethnicity categories (African American, American Indian, Asian/Pacific Islander, Latino, and White), each of three categories reported (learning disability, emotional disturbance, and mental retardation), and the total number enrolled.

The second source of data was the common core of data (CCD) (National Center for Educational Statistics 2000), including previous studies that compiled demographic and fiscal data of every public school and district in the United States into a list made available to the public. Variables collected were as follows:

a. Percentage of children in the community who have limited English proficiency
b. Median income of housing value of the community
c. Median income of households in the community with children
d. Percentage of adults in the community who have twelfth-grade education or less without a diploma

e. Percentage of children who are at risk
   f. Percentage of student enrollment identified as having a disability

The third source of data was district-level achievement date, which the researchers collected from fifty states and the District of Columbia. The form of these data was the percentage of students from each racial/ethnic category passing each subject at each grade level.

The result showed that both Latinos and African Americans performed much lower than white students in reading, science, math, and general knowledge in fourth, eighth, and twelfth grades. These scores were present even if the income and/or housing of the parent(s) was at a comfortable to average range. Race—along with academic performance, economics, and demography—played a great part in determining eligibility for the special programs. Although more than 77 percent of African Americans did not live in poverty, more African American students were eligible than any other ethnic group. The average achievement differences between groups of students would have led to disproportionate rates of identification even if the processes of referral, assessment, and certification were nonbiased (Hosp and Reschly 2004).

Conversely, Overton, Fielding, and Simonson (2004) found out that eligibility requirements for culturally and linguistically diverse learners were difficult and inconsistent. Because federal regulations required the use of unbiased assessment measures and techniques, they determined that assessors needed to be more qualified to determine the future of disadvantaged children. As cited in Overton et al. (2004), Gerstan and Woodward found that in some urban areas, students from linguistically diverse backgrounds were not referred for fear of possible legal action.

Overton et al. (2004) based the information they collected on hypothetical case studies about how eligibility decisions were made by the assessment personnel who routinely evaluated students from culturally and linguistically diverse backgrounds for learning disabled (LD) in one school system. They wanted to find out whether assessment personnel would defer making eligibility decisions with incomplete data. The primary focus was to collect information about the types of eligibility decisions made and the frequency with which assessors would defer making decisions when data were incomplete and the reasons given by them for their decisions. The participants included assessment personnel of 7 countries and 39 school systems on 432 campuses.

In the school systems, there were 43,273 public school staff members of which 86% were of Hispanic origin and 13% were of European American, Asian/Pacific Islander, or American Indian descent. Of the total enrollment, 95% had Spanish surnames and all the counties classified as economically depressed. Eighty-one percent of the students were from families classified as low income. Student population was broken down as follows: 10% in special education; 26% in bilingual programs; 11% in English as a second language (ESL); and 11% classified as immigrants. The participants in the case studies received questionnaires. The result showed that there was overrepresentation of children of Hispanic origin in the categories of learning disabilities, hearing impairments, and orthopedic impairments based on insufficient data supplied to the assessors. In addition, there was no assessment or placement of students who might have needed special education services because of fear of legal action (Overton et al. 2004).

Sager (2004) corroborated the research done by Overton et al. (2004) and Hosp and Reschly (2004). He highlighted the racial gap and divide among blacks, Latinos, and whites. He claimed that 15% of Albany's (New York) minority children passed the state math and English tests in comparison to 60% of the whites.

A study by a U.S. panel done in 2007 corroborated the previous studies indicating the overrepresentation of blacks classified as special education students. The U.S. Civil Rights Commission used the data collected from the U.S. Department of Education to sift through issues railed about including parental choice, school official judgment calls on special education placement, and effective early childhood education.

The data collected in 2006 racial makeup of the special education population indicated some of the disparities and higher representations of minority students in the overall student enrollment including the following:

- They were often placed in self-contained classrooms and given instruction that wasn't as rigorous as the curriculum offered to other students.
- Many minority students never graduated from high school.
- They were more likely to be found in the "judgmental" disability categories that requires some degree of subjectivity on the part of a school-based team in the evaluation process in learning disabilities, mental retardation, and emotional disturbance.

The panel's findings accrued, piggybacked on information from a 1992 survey, which showed that although black students made up about 16% of the total U.S. student population, about 32% of the students classified as mildly mentally retarded and 22% of the students diagnosed with emotional and behavioral disturbances were black. As evidenced, those disparities continue until today.

Additionally, a report (2007) also demonstrated that minority students in predominantly white school districts were significantly more at risk of being placed in special education than those in predominantly minority districts. However, according to the report, white parents fought like cats and dogs to get their children in special education classes for the attention and services. Whereas special education in more affluent areas was seen as a set of services that were provided to a child in a general education classroom, the opposite was true for others. In most less affluent or minority districts, special education was recognized as a special placement that took a child out of the regular classroom (Samuels 2007).

Similarly, Viadero (2008), in the article "Get Real on Race," confirmed some of the disparities emerging in the education of minority students. The report affirmed that minority students roamed the halls of their school "unimpeded" while their peers sat in class. "Colormuteness," the description of minority students wandering the halls, was widely observed by peers, security, administrators, and teachers who refused to address or curb the behavior. This practice exacerbated racial inequalities on a whole. Some of the reasons for the inaction on the part of personnel and staff included the following:

- Generic advice should be color blind to celebrate diversity.
- They didn't want researchers giving vague advice.
- Skepticism about race was at the forefront of educators' minds in every aspect of school business.
- Addressing the issue could reinforce stereotyping and be counterproductive.

The researchers also surmised that teachers of different races and different generations did not know how to accommodate these students. Though the teachers operated with the best intentions, the impact on the minority students was negative.

For instance, when the teachers grouped students academically for the benefit of the class, the minority students felt stigmatized. One student described that tracking this way, "you try to get all the black kids away from each other before [they] cause a nuclear holocaust." Similarly, when the minority students were placed with higher-achieving white students, the black students were often relegated to roles that gave them little or no opportunity to demonstrate or build their academic skills. One contributor to Viadero's research further asserted that the minority students felt left out when their questions were never answered but put off continuously.

The frustrated students believed that they were in a stereotyped group where the teachers' motivation to help became suspect.

Nonetheless, when whites entered a school situation, they were assured that "teachers here believe in [them]." In other words, race relations was a troublesome and painful issue, especially when minority students blatantly walked the halls while school personnel, security, and others ignored them. The teachers not only avoided the hall wanderers issue, but they also cast blame on the students, their values, and their families.

In the meantime, they failed to recognize that they contributed to the situation by ejecting African American students from their classroom, then neglecting to inform or alert security and school personnel. Eventually, these students were added as eligible for assessment.

Although the deinstitutionalization process and state and federal mandates were compelling administrators and teachers to make these children feel normal, the law does not demand placement of all disabled students in regular classrooms. Rather, on a case-by-case basis that placement is in a "least restrictive environment" (Including the Disabled Student, n.d.).

Mainstreaming

One of the least restrictive environments is mainstreaming. Adrian Harte (2004) explained it this way: "With the passage of Americans with Disabilities Act (1990), many heralded it as a complete victory in the last battle for full citizenship and full protection under the law. Legislation can smooth the way but positive attitudes and knowledge of disabilities will enable us all to live in an inclusive world" (Disabilities Awareness, 7, 2).

Mainstreaming began in the 1970s. It started as an educational method that included many different kinds of learners in the same classroom instead of separating students according to their learning disabilities. In the classrooms, students with disabilities and those who did not have disabilities were working together. This also included gifted students. The purpose for bringing all these students together was to give every student a typical classroom experience. Many changes and adjustments accommodated a variety of learners in one classroom. In such classrooms, teachers and aides used special teaching methods. They separated kids into groups, put some at different learning stations, and had independent tutoring time. Extraspecialized materials and equipment were all included. Besides, the trained teachers organized different activities for different students at all times (Mainstreaming in Classrooms, n.d.).

Seltzer (2000) reported that mainstreaming was for academics as well as for socialization for the special-needs children. He emphasized that success in mainstreaming was negligible. For example, he stated, children with Asperger's syndrome who were not usually invited out would derive much success by being included in a mainstreamed class with nondisabled students. However, the reporter cautioned that despite the success in mainstreaming, there were pitfalls in the implementation.

Mainstreaming, the teaching of many different students in one classroom at the same time, soon generated many questions about the effect of such integration on the nondisabled student. One researcher conducted a study to find out. The study was a story about a physically disabled boy who read to twenty-eight fourth-grade children in a mainstreamed classroom and twenty-nine nonmainstreamed children. The memory recognition task following the reading included ten characteristics attributed to the disabled boy in the story (acquisition items) and eight novel characteristics (distracter items). The number of errors made in the memory task reflected the extent to which the acquisition and distractor items were compatible with the mainstreamed and nonmainstreamed subjects' stereotype of the disabled. The results showed that the mainstreamed participants made significantly fewer errors on the recognition memory test (Lehrer, n.d.).

According to some reports, the mainstreaming process had some problems. Seltzer (2004) cautioned that many school programs focused on finance and student costs rather than on children in need. Therefore, more interest placed on cutting measures over student needs was within the realities of mainstreaming.

Many people became concerned about the effect of mainstreaming on regular students as well as special education students. The concerns included too much time devoted to special-needs children while depriving the nondisabled children quality time. In a survey sponsored by the American Federation of Teachers (AFT), 60 percent of the teachers surveyed said that they could not devote enough time to special education students. Forty-seven percent said that they could not pay enough attention to other students. The report concluded that mainstreaming was a poor policy and lofty ideal where special education and regular education students appeared to be victims (Including the Disabled Student, n.d.). This supported the findings of Paul, Turnbull, and Cruickshank (1977) where they found that the success of mainstreaming was dependent on cooperation, willingness, and capabilities of educators, students, parents, and the community.

Blankenship and Lily (1981) too viewed mainstreaming as a challenge or a nuisance. They found that in some cases mainstreaming was used as an excuse for cutting budgets and eliminating needed special education programs. They described the three factors crucial to successful mainstreaming as (1) the building and district administrators, (2) the knowledgeable special educators, and (3) the trained and qualified special classroom teacher—the most important factor.

In their research, Strain and Kerr (1981) also found that many regular classroom teachers had no access to or experience with applied behavior analysis literature on academic interventions. They stressed the need for researchers to focus more attention on the critical methodological issues of target behavior or selection, population description, and systematic evaluation of children's performance in order to maximize effective mainstreaming.

Inclusion

The other least restrictive environment is inclusion. Full inclusion meant that all students, regardless of disability or the severity of it, would be in a regular classroom or program, full time, where they would receive full services. Inclusion did not appear in the text of the statute or the implementing of regulations. Instead, the law requires that children with disabilities be educated to the maximum extent appropriate in the "least restrictive environment" that was interpreted by IDEA to mean regular education classroom (Special Education inclusion, n.d.).

To ensure the inclusion of special students in regular classroom, IDEA required the individual education plan (IEP) team to consider placement in the regular education classroom as the starting point of the educational process for special-needs children education process. In case the team determined that the regular education classroom was not the appropriate placement, then the team must include an explanation as to the contrary.

When questions as to the scope of inclusion surfaced, the courts stepped in to give the answers. *Greer v. Rome City School District* (Eleventh Circuit Court, 1992), *Sacramento City Unified School District v. Holland* (Ninth Circuit Court, 1994), and *Oberti v. Board of Education of the Borough of Clementon School District* (Third Circuit Court, 1993) all ruled in favor of the child to be included in a regular education classroom. Nevertheless, in *Poolaw v. Parker Unified School District* (Federal District Court, Arizona, 1994), the court found that regular education placement was not appropriate for the child (Special Education Inclusion, n.d.; Including the Disabled Student, n.d.).

Similarly, many parents were concerned about the segregation of the disabled children from their nondisabled peers. Sometimes the children were bussed to other communities that provided the services required for the disabled. This was in violation of the section of IDEA that specifically stated that the child should be educated in the school where such child would attend if nondisabled. However, IDEA allowed for supplementary aids and services with no clear explanation of the term, permitting schools and parents to interpret the term to their own determination (Steedman 2005).

All indications as to the effectiveness of the inclusion program were promising and positive as evidenced from a study called Success for All done at St. John's University with inner-city children. The program was a comprehensive effort that involved family support teams, professional development for teachers, reading, tutoring, special reading programs, eight-week reading assessments, and expanded opportunities for preschool and kindergarten children.

To assess the effectiveness of the Success for All program, researchers compared a control group with students in the program. Students with disabilities were included in first, second, and third grades. Comparisons included Woodcock Language Proficiency Battery (1984), Durrell Analysis of Reading Difficulty (1980), and Student Retention and Attendance. There was noticeable improvement in all areas, with the most dramatic occurring among the lowest achievers. Although these inner-city schools had normally high retention problems, only 4% of the fourth graders in the experimental group had been held back one or more grades, while the five control schools had 31% who had failed at least one year.

The research on the Success for All program demonstrated that with early and continuing intervention instead of remediation later, nearly all children would be successful in reading and social interactions. However, despite all the positive effectiveness of inclusion, one of its biggest issues was how to make it work well (Special Education inclusion, n.d.).

Although many schools implemented inclusion, there was no comprehensive or national data available on the special education students' academic gains, graduation rates, preparation for postsecondary schooling, and work or involvement in community living (Special Education inclusion, n.d.).

Conflicts/Implementation

The aforementioned problems in assessment, testing, mainstreaming, placement, finance, funding, and, most of all, interpretation of mandates have generated many different strategies in implementing appropriate and effective teaching and rehabilitation of the disabled. Such findings confirmed an earlier report by Van Osdol and Perryman (1974), who claimed that there was irreparable harm done to misplaced, improperly tested disabled students. This, they explained, came about because the school experience did not motivate these students but instead placed them in stressful situations comparable to "burial grounds" inadequate to meet the needs of the students.

This confirmed a previous study by McNamara (1998), who affirmed that there was no single right method used with success when rehabilitating or educating the disabled.

Since the mandates were broad and nonspecific, causing many different interpretations for implementation (PL 94-142 IDEA 2005), many school districts modified certain segments of the mandates to meet their needs. Researchers continued to demonstrate the lack of proper guidelines of the mandate. Davis (2004) declared that some teachers were not eager to acquire the required qualifications under the No Child Left Behind Act because of a lack of coordination at the federal level. Moreover, Olsen (2004) claimed that the accountability requirements posed unique challenges for the students and respective schools, resulting in the federal special education law coming in direct conflict with the No Child Left Behind Act. State changes in testing modifications with uncertainty of impact on results were included in the report.

Similarly, the American Federation of Teachers (AFT) in its February 2005 publications of *Capitol Watch* supported the report on broad laws in the article "President Signs Special Education Law." The article stated that the president signed a new phase of IDEA, giving schools more flexibility on how they could discipline special students. According to the article, schools could remove students who inflicted serious bodily injury to an alternative setting for up to forty-five school days. Nevertheless, this did not give principals more authority to remove dangerous or persistently disruptive students.

Furthermore, the same phase of the law imposed new sets of requirements for highly qualified teachers. These new requirements posed great concerns for special education teachers who might have had to meet separate requirements for each subject they teach. This new phase of IDEA also included more flexibility in the form of a high objective uniform state standard of evaluation (HOUSSE), which allowed veteran teachers to demonstrate their qualifications by means other than a test. They received the money but no specified time for them to meet the requirements.

Eleven Different Districts

The report of conflicting laws and mandates, implementation and interpretation problems, challenges posed for educators and teachers, parents and community concerns, and other issues allowed this to explore the ramifications in school districts in New York. For purposes of this paper, through direct observations, interviews, and, in some instances, working for more than five years, the researcher investigated eleven school districts—A through K—and compared, contrasted, and looked for other variables that made a difference in the educating of students with disabilities. For the academic setting of the districts, A-K, the researcher retrieved the necessary information from NYSED and conducted the exploration and profile of the district in the fall and spring of the school year 2004-2005.

Profile of Eleven (A-K) School Districts in New York

District A

This district is located in New York City (South Brooklyn). It is a district with high student needs with almost eight thousand students with an attendance rate of 81%. The reports are the dropout rate is 38%, suspension rate is 45%, and police incidence is 20.7%. Student ethnicity is as follows: Blacks, 75%; Hispanics, 20%; American Indians, Alaskans, Asians, or Pacific Islanders, 5%. This is a district with high student needs in relation to district resources. There are three elementary and three intermediate schools. One high school serves many local districts. Students must be qualified to enter specialized high schools.

Special education is classified as MIS 1 for LD (learning disabled students), MIS 11 = EH (emotionally handicapped students), MIS V = mentally retarded and autistic students, and SIS = resource room. This district assesses the students prior to entering the intermediate or middle school. But typical for this district, services begin in the middle school. In this district, there are not more than twelve special education students in a class. There is one inclusion class with two teachers—one general education and one special education teacher. There is no aide or paraprofessional.

The students are extremely low functioning. Although the school observed is not elementary, the students have difficulty recognizing or decoding sight vocabulary for the second and third grades. However, the policy of the district is to promote the children with their class whether they pass or not. In addition, some special education staff members, including teachers working in the program, are unqualified. Nevertheless, these teachers write the IEP without anyone else's input or supervision.

When questioned about the implementation and compliance of special education rules and regulations, many teachers simply replied, "No one checks." The special students receive IEP certificates, but they are not required to participate in any of the graduation ceremonies. In this district, special education classrooms are the only ones located in the basement of the building.

Less than 10% of the families are homeowners. The district provides free or reduced lunch to the entire student population. The median income is approximately $25,000-$30,000. Almost 93% of the district population is on public assistance. Less than 10% of the student population moves to higher academia.

District B

This district is located in east Nassau County. The total enrollment is over 6,400 students with an attendance rate of 94.2%. Student suspension is 1.7%, dropout rate is 0%. Student ethnicity is American Indian, Alaskan, Asian, or Pacific Islander, 14.4%; black (non-Hispanic), 0.3%; Hispanic, 1.8%; white (non-Hispanic), 83.5%. Percentage of students with disabilities is at 1.8%, while the economically disadvantaged is at 0%. There are ten schools in this district. There are seven elementary, two middle, and one high school.

More than 90% of the families in the district have a median income of $100,000-$125,000. The district provides free or reduced lunch to 0.4% of the student population. The district is a low student needs in relation to district resource capacity.

Special education services begin at the elementary level with resource services such as speech and language, reading, occupational therapy, physical therapy, and any other special services included. There is also a special program for autistic children where the child-to-aide ratio is 1:1. Moreover, there is a well-stocked resource room with two teachers and two assistants. Although the resource room is well stocked and staffed, it also has access to the library and a separate testing area. In the resource room, there are learning stations set up where students receive as much help as needed. Also, the class sizes and children in self-contained mainstreamed classes are not more than ten students when and where possible during the day.

At the middle school, there are self-contained and inclusion classes as well as resource services that are an extension of the services provided at the elementary level. The school holds students to high standards both in behavior and in academic achievement. There is a collaborative, communicative, and cooperative atmosphere among the teachers.

At the high school, the special education classrooms are in a separate wing of the large school. Students are either self-contained or they receive resource room services. They are very much a part of the school as are the teachers. There is a director of pupil personnel services as well as a chairperson at the high school and each middle school. More than 90% of the special students receive Regents diplomas and go on to college.

District C

This is a district with low student needs located in south Nassau County. The student enrollment is about 1,300 with an attendance rate of 95.8%, dropout rate of 0.0%, and student suspension rate of 0.9%. Student ethnicity: American Indians, Alaskans, Asians, Pacific Islanders, 1.6%; Blacks, 0.9%; Hispanics, 2.7%; Whites, 94.8%; students with disabilities, 1.7%.

About 92% of families in this district have an annual income of more than $150,000 with 99% owning single-family homes. The school provides free or reduced lunch to 2.7% of the student population.

There are three elementary schools, two middle schools, and three high schools here. Special education services begin from grade 1, where there are inclusion classes. Almost all the special children are in inclusion classes. By the time the students reach high school, they do not need special education classes.

District D.

This is a low-student-needs district located in mid-Nassau County. Total enrollment is over 2,700 with an attendance rate of 96%, suspension rate of 1.3%, and dropout rate of 0.3%. Student ethnicity is American Indian, Alaskan, Asian, or Pacific Islander, 2.3%; blacks (non-Hispanic), 0.5%; Hispanic, 2.5%; and whites (non-Hispanic), 94.7%. Percentage of students with disabilities is at 0.66%.

There are two elementary schools, one middle school, and one high school in the district. Parochial schools utilize the special education services in the district. Over 90% of the families have a median income of $130,000-$150,000, with home ownership of 95%. The district provides free or reduced lunch to 2.5% of the student population.

The only self-contained programs in the district are life skills classes. The students get language, speech, occupational therapy, physical therapy, and counseling as needed. The limit at the high school is 12:12. They stay in school until age twenty-one or until they can be self-sufficient. Some of them attend the Board of Cooperative Educational Services (BOCES) where individuality is addressed specifically. This program allows for the students to learn a trade or marketable skills such as culinary arts, air-conditioning, refrigeration and heating, aircraft maintenance, animal skills, auto mechanics, child development services, carpentry, computer business operations, construction, computer repair, cosmetology, electronics, fashion technology, nurse assisting, medical office technology, political science, plumbing and heating, rehabilitation aid, travel and tourism, and welding without having to attend college. They also go as a class to computers, technology education, art, and adaptive education in the home school. They attend a ten-minute homeroom daily with the general education population. A special education teacher accompanies them when they participate in general education activities. There is a special room adjoining their class for time-out as needed. Special students who need the services the most are part of the inclusion model with coteaching. The special education teacher is responsible for modifying assignments and tests for the special children. Depending on their IEPs, the teacher takes them out of the class for testing. Both teachers are responsible for the content area, and they plan together.

The inclusion students usually have a support period daily, three times a week in a special quiet carpeted room. The special education teachers share a room with one other special teacher. Some students only have resource services two, three, or five times a week in the special education classrooms. Other students receive only math or reading. Only 10% of the students have serious academic problems, and 11% need extra help to do the Regents successfully. As a result, over 74% of the students receive Regents diplomas.

District E

This district is located in south Nassau, with a student enrollment of more than 2,400 and an attendance rate of 96%. It is a low student needs district with 1% of the students having serious academic problems and 5% needing extra help to pass the Regents exams. Student ethnicity is American Indian, Alaskan, Asian, or Pacific Islander, 4.4%; blacks (non-Hispanic), 2.8%; Hispanic, 3.3%; and whites, 89.5%. Over 85% of the families are homeowners, having a median income of $95,000-$120,000. The district provides free or reduced lunch to 4.3% of the student population.

There are six elementary schools, two middle schools, and one high school in the district. Self-contained classrooms are in the elementary right through the high school level. There is not a great demand for special education services in the high school because of the intensity of the programs at the lower levels. All the special teachers work in conjunction with the general education teachers to help the students achieve. Resource and special services are available as needed and 99% of the students receive Regents diplomas at the end.

District F.

This district is located in West Suffolk County. It is an average-student-needs district with student enrollment of more than 6,400. The attendance rate is 85% and dropout rate is 5%. Student ethnicity is blacks, 6%; Hispanic, 9%; Asian, Alaskan, or American Indian, 4%; and whites, 80%. Percentage of students with disabilities is at 14.8%.

About 60% of the families have an annual household income of $85,000-$100,000, with less than 10% earning $50,000-$80,000. The district provides free or reduced lunch to 25% of the student population.

There are six schools—four elementary, one junior, and one senior high school—in this district. There is a push-in and pullout ESL as well as a special education kindergarten program in the elementary schools. When there is a push-in, the ESL teacher leads the class for that period. Some students have a 1:1 aide-to-student ratio. There are two teachers at all times in the inclusion and mainstream classes. Other students receive only resource services in reading, while some receive pullout service for language.

At the middle school, there are self-contained classes for special education students. However, all the special students receive mainstream services for some subjects throughout the day and for art, music, and physical education as well. The self-contained classes have two teachers, and the student-to-aide ratio is 1:2, with not more than twelve students to a class. The special education department is in one wing of the school.

At the high school, the same services extend from the middle school. However, the eleventh and twelfth graders require less service because they attend vocational education programs at BOCES. Teachers and students are at a high achievement level in computer skills in this district. Students who are absent, in in-school suspension, or other are responsible for all work missed. Students observe all school rules and regulations as outlined. Administrators and mentor teachers who create an ongoing written and visual portfolio observe and evaluate the teachers.

District G.

This is a high-student-needs district located in north Nassau County. The student enrollment is more than 3,700. The attendance rate is 90%; dropout rate, 4.3%; student suspension, 8.1%; and students with serious academic problems, 9.8%. Student ethnicity is American Indian, Alaskan, Asian, or Pacific Islander, 1.9%; blacks (non-Hispanic), 50.0%; Hispanic, 46.4%; and whites, 1.8%. Percentage of students with disabilities is at 26%, while the economically disadvantaged is at 69%.

Less than 50% of the families are homeowners and have an annual household income of $50,000-$95,000. About 20% earn $30,000-$45,000, and 10% earn less than $30,000. The district provides free or reduced lunch to 84% of the student population.

In this district, there are six schools—one high school, one middle school, and four elementary schools. ESL classes, both self-contained and pullout programs, are at the elementary level. Each of these classes has an aide who works three to four hours per day with the special students.

Testing and assessment begins at the middle school level. Students who need special services are mostly in self-contained classes of more than fifteen students with a part-time aide. They receive services such as speech, counseling, and language and ESL classes. This level also has its own department chair.

At the high school level, there are two inclusion classes as well as self-contained classes. There are also beginning (new students) and intermediate ESL classes. One special education teacher works with the two inclusion classes of fifteen to twenty-five students. Neither of the classes has an aide to assist the teachers for skills period.

Special education teachers teach where and when there is available space to accommodate regular teachers. Resource service teachers work out of rolling carts with few resources. Some special education teachers have part-time aides while others have none. At times teachers and students cannot communicate because of language barriers. Several special-needs children go to BOCES at the eleventh—or twelfth-grade level. Special students hardly participate in the general education activities. About 70% of them drop out at or before the twelfth grade while others receive a local diploma or IEP certificate. Although there is an open-door policy in this district, special-needs children hardly utilize it.

District H.

This district is a low-student-needs district with an enrollment of more than 7,600 students. The attendance rate is 94.4%; dropout rate, 0.1%; and student suspension rate, 2.1%. It is located in southwest Nassau County. Student ethnicity is American Indian, Alaskan, Asian, or Pacific Islander, 1.8%; blacks, 2%; Hispanics, 7.0%; and whites, 89.1%. Percentage of students with disabilities is at 12%. Four percent of the students have serious academic deficiencies, and 48% need extra help to meet Regents requirements. More than 70% of the families have a median annual income of $95,000-$120,000. Fifteen percent earn $70,000-$90,000, and 10% earn less than $50,000. The district provides free or reduced lunch to the student population.

In this district, there are seven elementary schools, one junior, and one senior high school. At the elementary level, the special-needs children receive all the resources and services they require. There are teachers and full-time aides assigned to small classes to provide whatever the students need.

By the time the students get to the middle school, they have a routine in place. There are self-contained as well as inclusion classes. All the self-contained students receive mainstreamed classes throughout the day. The classes are small with not more than twelve students with a 1:2 student-to-aide ratio. There is a chairperson for the middle school.

There is a director of pupil personnel services and a chairperson for the high school where the chairperson has no instructional class periods. He or she devotes the time making sure that the special education department is in compliance in all areas and observes, helps, and encourages the teachers. The students attend self-contained as well as mainstreamed classes in the high school. Inclusion classes are math, science, English, and social studies from grades nine to twelve, with an inclusion teacher for each grade level and subject. Two inclusion teachers share a classroom for support. The students in the ninth and tenth grades have daily support that decreases in the eleventh and twelfth grades. Many of these students attend BOCES for vocational education.

In this model, content area teachers do most of the teaching, and the inclusion teachers focus on the behavior and comprehension of materials. They are also available at all times to help students who need it. Self-contained teachers, resource teachers, and inclusion teachers work as a team in one suite. They collaborate, communicate, and cooperate in the interests of the students. The students also have access to a computer lab and are eager to learn. More than 90% of these special-needs students obtain a Regents diploma and go on to college.

District I.

This is a high-student-needs district located in East Brooklyn with 70% attendance rate; dropout rate, 20%; and suspension rate, 25%. Student enrollment is about 9,000. Student ethnicity is Asians, American Indians, Alaskan, Pacific Islanders, 2.0%; blacks (non-Hispanic), 80%; and Hispanics (non-white), 18%. Percentage of students with disabilities is at 85%, with police incidents at 79%. About 70% of the families are welfare recipients. Less than 10% have an annual income of less than $40,000 and are homeowners. The district provides free lunch to 99% of the student population.

There is no official identification or classification of special students at the elementary schools. All the students work in their respective classes and go on to higher levels together as a group.

The district classifies special-needs students at the junior and high school level where they are self-contained in classes of fifteen or more students. There is a full-time paraprofessional with each self-contained teacher, and the students are mainstreamed for physical education, lunch, art, and music. Less than 50% of the students move on to the high school level.

At the high school level, it is a similar setup, with self-contained classes and a full-time paraprofessional. The students and their parents move several times annually, allowing little follow-through or continuity of their education. Vocational education is available to these students only if they choose a high school that has such programs. Furthermore, the high schools that offer such programs accept students with a certain level of IQ. Usually, special-needs students are not qualified. Most of the students do not know their guidance counselor. The teachers write the IEPs with no input from the parents, social workers, or other personnel. After the completion of the IEP, a copy is mailed to 25% of the parents.

District J.

This is a low-student-needs district located in southwest Nassau with an enrollment of more than 2,700 students. Attendance rate is 95%; suspension rate, 4%; and dropout rate, 0.9%. Student ethnicity is American Indians, Alaskans, Asians, or Pacific Islanders, 6.0%; blacks (non-Hispanic), 2.7%; Hispanics, 12.6%; and whites, 78.8%. Percentage of students with disabilities is at 2.8%. More than 80% of the families have a median annual income of $100,000-$180,000 and have their own single family home. The district provides free or reduced lunch to 12% of the student population.

There are seven schools in the district—five elementary, one junior high, and one senior high school. This district starts to address special-needs children at the elementary level. The students receive self-contained and resource services. Each special-needs student has a teacher and a full-time aide.

The district provides inclusion and mainstreamed classes for special students at the middle and high school level. The support system in place helps the students where the classes do not exceed twelve students. There is a resource room, testing room, and computer lab available to them. The teachers work as a team—general, special, inclusion, and self-contained teachers.

By the time the students reach the eleventh and twelfth grades, they do not need as many services. The students can attend vocational education programs at BOCES. They work with their teachers cooperatively, who reward them accordingly. More than 85% of the students obtain a Regents diploma.

District K

This is a low student needs district located in mideast Suffolk County with student enrollment of more than 1,200. The ethnicity of the student is as follows: American Indians, Alaskans, Asians, or Pacific Islanders, 8.1%; Blacks (non-Hispanic), 10.2%; Hispanics, 3.9%; Whites (non-Hispanic), 77.8%; students with disabilities, 2.2%.

More than 90% of the families have a median income of $122,000-$159,999 with 99% as owners of single-family homes. The district provides free or reduced lunch to 6.8% of the student population.

The school district is comprised of seven elementary schools, two junior and two senior high schools. This district starts intervention with special-needs children at the elementary level, where there are special education teachers, resource service teachers, counselors, occupational and physical therapists (OT and PT), and speech and language providers. However, this district does not classify the students until middle school.

At the middle school, the service providers are available on-site. Special-needs students are in self-contained classes but mainstreamed for more than 35% of the day.

At the high-school level, special needs students are in self-contained classes but mainstreamed for more than 50% of the day. The students have access to computer labs and a quiet room and special service rooms set up for that population. Less than 10% of the students are in inclusion classes with a special education teacher and a full-time aide. There is a skills period where the educators help the students on a one-to-one basis. Every special education teacher has a full-time aide. The inclusion and self-contained classes have ten students maximum. Many eleventh and twelfth graders attend vocational education programs. The teachers work together as a team and have high expectations for their students. Over 85% of the students receive a Regents diploma and go on to college.

Examining the Factors

The following tables show the factors and variables that the researcher uncovered from the investigation of the eleven school districts, A-K.

Table 1

Teachers and service providers are the personnel directly involved with the students in the education process. This does not include custody, cafeteria, or security service workers.

District	Average Median Annual Income (U.S. $)	No. of Teachers and Service Providers	% of Fully Licensed Teachers	Student Population
A	25,000	345	46.8	8,500
B	112,500	824	98.8	6,472
C	160,000	152	99.0	1,313
D	140,000	301	99.0	2,718
E	107,500	209	95.0	2,435
F	102,500	654	90.0	6,502
G	75,000	440	89.0	4,000
H	175,000	735	98.0	7,622
I	40,000	389	48.9	9,100
J	125,000	421	96.0	2,717
K	150,000	1,042	99.1	9,192

Table 2

Comparison of minority students with percentage of students qualified for free Or reduced lunch.

District	% of Black Students	% of Spanish Students	Suspension Rate	Drop Out Rate	Attendance Rate	% of free Lunch
A	75.00	20.00	45.00	38.00	81.00	93.70
B	0.30	1.80	1.70	—	94.20	0.40
C	0.90	2.70	0.90	—	95.80	2.70
D	0.50	2.50	1.30	0.30	95.70	2.50
E	2.80	3.30	0.70	—	96.10	4.30
F	6.00	9.00	5.40	5.00	85.00	20.50
G	50.00	40.00	9.10	4.30	94.20	83.40
H	2.00	7.00	2.10	0.10	94.40	6.70
I	80.00	18.00	25.00	25.00	75.00	98.20
J	2.70	12.60	4.00	0.90	95.10	12.00
K	10.20	3.90	2.70	0.40	95.40	6.80

Table 3

Comparison of the percentage of students with disabilities with the population of minority student population

District	% of Black Student Population	% of Spanish Students	Students' Needs	% of Students with Disabilities
A	75.00	20.00	high	25.00
B	0.30	1.80	low	1.80
C	0.90	2.70	low	1.70
D	0.50	2.50	low	0.50
E	2.80	3.30	low	2.10
F	6.00	9.00	average	14.80
G	50.00	40.00	high	26.00
H	2.00	7.00	low	12.00
I	80.00	18.00	high	30.00
J	2.70	12.60	low	2.80
K	10.20	3.90	low	2.20

Table 4

Suspension and dropout rates in correlation with the white population and the percentage of students with disabilities

District	% of White Student Population	% of Asian Students	Suspension Rate (%)	Dropout Rate (%)	% of Students with Disabilities
A	0.00	5.00	45.00	38.00	25.00
B	83.50	14.00	1.70	0.00	1.80
C	94.80	1.60	0.90	0.00	1.70
D	94.70	2.30	1.30	0.30	0.50
E	89.50	4.40	0.70	0.00	2.10
F	80.00	4.00	5.40	5.00	14.80
G	1.80	1.90	9.10	4.30	26.00
H	89.10	1.80	2.10	0.10	12.00
I	0.15	0.50	25.00	25.00	30.00
J	78.80	6.00	4.00	0.90	2.80
K	77.80	8.10	2.70	0.40	2.20

Table 5

The average median income as it correlates to the percentage of licensed teachers, minority and special needs students

District	Median Income	% of Minority Students	% of Special Needs	% Licensed Teachers
A	$25,000.00	95.00	25.00	46.8
B	$112,500.00	2.10	1.80	98.8
C	$160,000.00	3.60	1.70	99
D	$140,000.00	3.00	0.50	99
E	$107,500.00	6.10	2.10	95.09
F	$102,500.00	15.00	14.80	90
G	$75,000.00	90.00	26.00	89
H	$175,000.00	9.00	12.00	98
I	$40,000.00	98.00	30.00	48.1
J	$125,000.00	15.30	2.80	96
K	$150,000.00	14.20	2.20	99.15

The present researcher incorporated information from the report card issued by the State Education Department (SED) in 2004 and compared the findings, in Figure 1 and Figure 2.

Figure 1

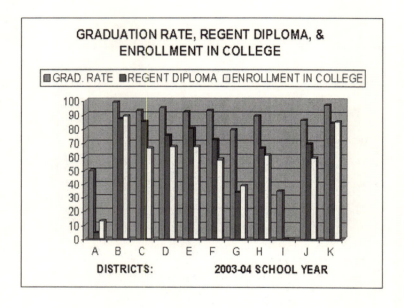

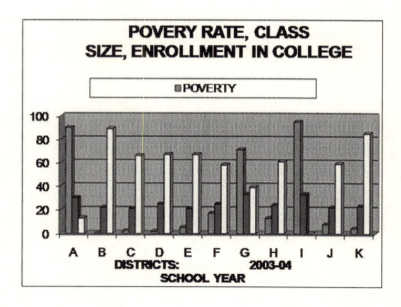

Discussion

Districts B, D, and K have a high graduation rate with more than 75% receiving Regents diplomas. This investigation showed that the respective students received intense help and persistent troubleshooting by teachers, administrators, and service providers. Students receive close monitoring with extra help from a considerable team effort among the staff personnel. Other factors presumably played a significant role in the success of the students in these districts. This also occurred with Griffin (1988) who had signified that social class, socioeconomic status, persistence in school, test scores, and grades attainment or achievement were closely associated with educational success. But with all the efforts put forth by laws, court decisions, and advocates for equal education, the research indicated that race played, and continues today, a significant role in the success and/or failure of a student.

It is now apparent that there are conflicts in attaining success. There is a greater suspension and dropout rate, fewer college-bound students, and higher rate of unlicensed teachers in districts with more disproportionate, minority special education students.

Updated investigation revealed further neglect of minority students who are allowed to wander the halls unimpeded through colormuteness.

Socioeconomics

From the eleven districts investigated, the researcher showed the median income of the families in each district as well as the percentage of special-needs children there. Wallace and McLoughlin (1988) found that economics had its limitations but influenced, nonetheless, the educational process and outcome of student achievement. Accordingly, economic deprivation limited the access to adequate educational exposure and service (Appalachia Education Laboratory 1996-2005). The International Covenant on Economics stressed the importance of proper care for mothers to prevent disabilities because economic conditions gave rise to infant disabilities to babies and promoted antisocial behaviors and family conflicts in the long run (Enable Human Rights and Disabled Persons 2003-2004).

4

MASKS UNVEILED

FUNDING

Equipping a classroom for appropriate and effective learning is analogous to a good tradesperson acquiring tools for his trade. Money becomes the catalyst in high-quality and job performances. Davis et al. (2005) discovered that the best results occurred in schools with the highest level of funding. They explained that children did better in schools where resources were available to provide supplementary aids. Another researcher found that the size and resources of a school district affected the distribution of necessary supplies and material that the student required. For that reason, a large school district with many resources usually invested more in services and support for the children (Steedman 1997-2001).

Bartolomeo (2004) acknowledged that New York State has had more than a decade of litigation brought about by parents and advocacy groups challenging the constitutionality of its school funding system. He emphasized that raising additional revenue was the only way to solve the litigation problems and that richer areas should fund the poorer areas. He concluded that there was a clear correlation between district's fiscal stability and state test scores.

Strachan (2004) also established that the achievement gap in New York State was shrinking very slowly. He went on to depict that "excellence would only be achieved if all school districts, particularly those in New York's big cities, poor rural and poor suburban areas where poverty was prevalent, had had sufficient resources."

Neira (2004) also demonstrated that funding problems were crucial to the educational process. She outlined a separate special education funding system with two components, which are the following:

- A base special education aide for students with disabilities. School districts would receive aid to support placement of student in a full continuum of services, including those provided in public schools, BOCES, and approved private schools.
- Aid for high-cost students with disabilities. Additional aid would be provided for students placed in high-cost public or private facilities.

New York State has been embroiled in numerous lawsuits dating back to 1993 in which the duration of resolution took away valuable time and money from districts that were most needy. The New York Civil Liberties Union filed a lawsuit claiming that New York was failing to provide proper education for children in twenty-seven schools and asked that state intervene and assist. The judge ruled that the state could not be asked to intervene at the local level and that any failures to provide a sound basic education must be addressed by the districts (Medina 2005). The decision followed a state supreme court decision ordering $5.6 billion in additional aid for New York City schools. This lawsuit also accused the state of failing to provide for basic education needs like textbooks and adequate buildings. This action enabled some schools to move forward while others were cautious in implementing or piloting new programs while fiscal wars enmeshed other students.

Consequently, the promise of improving special education remained unfulfilled because programs did not receive adequate funding. Congress has never lived up to its promise of 1975 that said that the federal government would provide 40 percent of the excess cost of educating students with disabilities. The federal government had delivered only a half of its promise (*Capitol Watch* 2005).

According to one researcher, funding that should have been allotted to all districts had been made into a game of the best results or a prized target. He cautioned that there was money earmarked toward student performances because "the push is on to link education spending to academic results." Thus, schools whose students performed at the highest levels of the goals set by the states and the No Child Left Behind gained top dollars. The report also averred that the concepts of inadequacy were applied to such groups as students with disabilities, those with limited English proficiency, and those reared in poverty. He maintained that there were adjustments made to the formulas that reflected cost of living differences between regions, the poor family, and the students' success level (Rose 2005).

Rose's report also depicted that any stage-led effort to guarantee adequate resources would be difficult to achieve without a matching federal commitment. Additionally, the NCLB Act has imposed costly requirements and changes without the dispensing of the fund promised as the law stated. Federal appropriations gave the NCLB $9.6 billion less than the amounts authorized by Congress, and Title I funding was $7.7 billion less than what the act promised. This left states and districts with huge unfunded mandates. Therefore, tight state budgets are forcing schools to do more with less.

In his report "Schools Sweating over Report Card," Hilderbrand (2005) declared that the state education department announced the result of testing in 125 districts across Long Island, New York, and more than seven hundred districts statewide. The report confirmed that schools where scores fell short of state and U.S. standards for two or more consecutive years faced official sanctions, including potential loss of federal financial aid. Medina (2005) acknowledged that tests scores decided the dissemination of funds, creating a "Robin Hood" approach.

The Robin Hood approach seemed unproductive as indicated by Merrow (2007). He illumined blatant loopholes in the learning process, encouraging statistical manipulation of academic progress meaningless or suspect. Although the 2001 legislation of President George W. Bush was well-intentioned, Merrow claimed that subgroups including low-income families, minority groups, and students with disabilities must make adequate yearly progress where they are pressured for test scores. Such action put school districts/testers in a difficult situation. Hypothetical scores, thus, become the norm, creating an uncomfortable situation for the student. Today, this scenario allows the states to make their own rules in regard to subgrouping, grading, number of students, no consistency or valid scoring.

Although the purpose of the NCLB was insightful, it was not broad enough, leaving diverse kids behind. Hoff in October 2007 declared that the problems of these diverse kids were not adequately addressed. Schools, he said, had been celebrating diverse cultures in isolation rather than integrating them into the whole school curriculum to reflect the ethnic, linguistic, and varied complementary experiences. This was counterproductive in a school system with the composition of the following:

— 60% of public schools—white
— 18% of public schools—Hispanics

— 16% of public schools—black
— 4% of public schools—Asian

Similarly, 22% of the students have at least one foreign-born parent, and 6% are foreign-born themselves, while 10 million speak a language other than English at home. Yet schools are culturally illiterate when addressing diverse issues.

According to Hoff (December 2007), NCLB had added problems where funding was shifted from "allocation of funding" to how to distribute money, overshadowing other policy discussions. Some flaws are as follows:

- The distribution of $12.8 billion Title I program for disadvantaged students benefited the nation's large cities as well as suburban areas with pockets of poverty.
- Districts with high enrollment and low poverty rates received more money per Title I pupil than districts with small enrollments and high poverty rates, leaving the neediest schools without funding.
- Legislation signed by President Bush in 2002 held schools accountable for increasing students' achievement for disadvantaged students who were not on pace to be proficient by the end of 2013-14 school year.
- Emphasis on closing the achievement gap between blacks and whites and Spanish and non-Spanish, creating environments for directing a greater portion of Title I funds to needy districts.

Although the funds were to be used to help the neediest districts, Congress spread the funds, instead, across school districts to schools with the highest poverty.

Accordingly, Hoff and Walsh (2008) explained that states were not clear on their financial obligations as they agreed to accept federal money under NCLB law. Despite the confusion of the mandates, states and districts were not mandated to use their own resources to comply with laws on testing and school improvements.

However, Hoff and Walsh (2008) indicated that states and districts were not relieved from using their own money to comply with the NCLB law as decided by the Sixth Circuit Court case. In the meantime, national education groups continued to lobby Congress for additional funds for disadvantaged students and received $25 billion to be spent on Title I.

Samuels (2008) described another group of students in need of funds, adding more confusion to the mandates of NCLB. Students with health or cognitive problems who are not eligible for services under Individuals with Disabilities Education Act (IDEA) have protection under another federal law, Section 504 of the Rehabilitation Act of 1973. Samuels reported that the laws posed many problems for administrators in evaluating students for Section 504 eligibility.

They complained that every child that is eligible for help under IDEA is also covered under Section 504, but not every Section 504 student is eligible for special education services; recent legal decisions suggested that a child who is not eligible for IDEA is likely not eligible for Section 504 accommodations either. Although once a child receives 504, he/she is eligible for many of the protections under IDEA. Even lawyers and advocates for parents, intimated Samuels, can be confused over the twist and turns of the laws.

Samuels continued to describe further problems with Section 504, where teachers in urban schools are unfamiliar with Section 504; but in suburban school(s), the term is common, leaving students in urban areas without service. Another problem that Samuels signified is the eligibility in which disability does not guarantee Section 504 services. If a child can be brought up to the standards of an average peer, the child is not eligible for Section 504 services. This is because students are measured against average peers, not against their potential.

Despite the ambiguity, Samuels observed that administrators would give accommodations as consolation "prizes" to students whose disabilities are not severe enough to qualify them for special education.

Resources

Inadequate funding impacted the ability to tap all resources necessary to affect a proficient educational program. Neufeldt and Guralnik (1997, 1996) explicated the meaning of resources as "something that lies ready for use or that can be drawn upon and to take care of a need and inner resource as the ability to deal promptly and effectively with problems and difficulties." They cautioned that underfunded school districts limited the efforts of administrators and teachers to encourage or start new programs.

Other investigation (Schwarz 1995) pointed out that new and updated technology, research projects, pilot programs, as well as expanded programs needed finances to expedite them. As a result, only inadequate skeletal programs remained after the elimination of vital school programs. The report also outlined that budget woes stopped all efforts to develop new plans. It also depicted that states took little action to develop teacher compensation plans, while others created their own pay-for-performance programs based on teacher acquisition of knowledge and skills.

Bartolomeo (2004) also demonstrated that several districts in New York had serious setbacks in education due to budget cuts where more than two hundred teachers lost their jobs at the start of the school year. The crisis prompted the Federation of Teachers to urge state and local lawmakers to help restore programs and personnel. Some districts in Buffalo closed schools and eliminated jobs, and approximately eight hundred teachers in New York City faced reassignment after having been "excessed from schools that lost state funding, leaving only programs that could boost the amount of funding to the particular district."

In addition, Tompkins (2008) apprised some complaints from rural communities especially in the poorest rural regions in which they detailed the following problems they faced continuously:

- Their top poverty issue is education.
- They are locked into miserly funding that keep rural teacher too low to compete with wealthy districts.
- Highly respected veteran teachers are badgered into early retirement by rules that label them unfairly for teaching a subject out of their field.
- Education is carried out in woeful facilities that let rain in and heat out.
- The tax policies imposed saddle the poorest people with the heaviest education tax load.
- The educational discipline is so racially charged that it put kids on the streets instead of in the classrooms.
- To consolidate schools, students succumb to inhumanely long bus rides only to be subjected to irrational curriculum requirements in thinly staffed schools operating on lean budgets.

Tompkins (2007) disclosed further that of the more than 26,000 rural communities, 23% are members of minority groups, which grew 55% from 1996 to 2005. Also of the 950,000 students served nationwide, 26% are African Americans, 32% are Title I students, 20% are Hispanics, and 10% are Native Americans. Based on an investigation of Rural 800 districts, Tompkins concluded that the "poorest rural students attend in the poorest states" with the least taxable resources to support an adequate education.

Politics

As Rose (2005), Bartolomeo (2004), Schwarz (1995), and other researchers uncovered, lack of funding impeded the ability to obtain needed resources for special children. Conversely, Medina (2005) and Schemo (2004) showed that politics also impacted the educational process of the disabled.

In his study, Schemo reported that Congress pared down rights and privileges that advocates won for the disabled through acts and laws such as PL 99-372. In its place, Congress gave state and school officials more power to shape the terms for providing services to the disabled. This, the report maintained, made it harder for unsatisfied parents to sue to obtain services for their disabled children. Instead, parents had to submit to mediation or other meetings to give school officials a last chance to resolve disputes before the courts intervened. In addition, if the disputes before the court deemed the suit frivolous or aimed at harassing a school system, the school districts recovered costs from parents and their lawyers.

Therefore, huge legal fees were written in the federal law. This, the report insisted, made it easier for school districts to do whatever they desired, making it more difficult for parents to protect the rights of their children. In addition, school districts had greater latitude to remove disabled children who misbehaved. The burden to prove that the child's disability caused the inappropriate behavior shifted from the school to the parent.

Similarly, Truscott et al. (2004) conducted an in-depth research and acquiesced with other reports about special education in educational reform. In the research, they discovered that U.S. educational reform ignored special education in the major restructuring of education. They contended that general education reforms perceived special education as a separate entity removed from ongoing reform efforts.

The report of the President's Commission on Excellence in Special Education (2002) previously attested to the finding of Truscott et al. (2004) when it confirmed that the de facto separation of special education from general education was a key concern and target for change. The researchers also indicated that educators recognized students with educational disabilities as the responsibility of general education, with special education provided as a supplementary rather than a separate service.

Other findings concluded that there was little or no connection between general and special education policy reform at the national level, making it difficult to perceive any meaningful collaboration occurring between special and general education in reforms designed to affect all classrooms. As a result, topics that affected special students were discussed with no reference to special education. Such actions occurred in districts where administrators expressed support for the inclusion of special education students in general education classes and activities (Truscott et al. 2004; Davis 2004).

However, Van Rockel (2008) affirmed that the public education system has allowed 50% of young African American and Hispanic males to be devoid of education because of politics.

Accountability

The political issues raised by the researchers Truscott, Davis, and Medina gave pause to the question of accountability. Olsen (2004) reported that the biggest concerns in addressing the shortcomings of the disabled were the reliability of tests administered to them. He claimed that tests did not accurately measure the performance of the students. Though states offered changes known as accommodations, there was no solid research signifying how the changes influenced the test results.

Additionally, the report acknowledged that the law's accountability requirements posed unique challenges for students with disabilities and the schools that served them, thus labeling schools as inadequate. Then, too, to measure the students' achievement meant that schools were judged based on the growth year to year and not just whether students met the absolute levels of performance. This determined how effective schools were in educating students with disabilities. As a result, some states set such high threshold that many schools were not reporting results for special education or LEP students (Olsen 2004).

Paglin (2004) also cautioned that instruction to special students was a recipe for disaster, particularly in low-income communities where transient hotels and homeless shelters are plentiful. Paglin indicated that evaluation teams referred kids to special education to make sure that they received instruction not available in the regular classroom where each school chose its own reading program. These actions gave rise to inconsistency from school to school, grade to grade, and room to room. Schools excluded disabled students from the accountability system when they used standardized tests to rate the schools' performance. Schools also opted instead to give them alternative exams that could be more open to manipulation. Besides, school officials outnumbered and silenced parents who insisted that their special children take graduate-level exam (Schemo 2004).

Gates (2005) demonstrated mounting evidence that depicted the education process inadequately trained many students, especially the disabled. He asserted that the nation was in peril because the school system failed the poor and minorities in the twenty-first century. He agreed with the findings of previous researchers that lack of accountability and resources (Andreatt 2004; Paglin 2004) caused the placement of the poor and minority in overcrowded classes. The students in such cases did not/could not succeed and remained unemployable. Gates also indicated that the arrest records for these dropouts rose four times more than those who remained in school and received their diploma. Others, he claimed, died young because of years of poor health care, unsafe living conditions, and violence. He also confirmed the findings of Schwarz (1995) who found that state mandates did not help students, especially special-needs students whose parents could not voice their opinion to school authorities.

Likewise, Gates reiterated the fact that millions of children never got a chance to fulfill the promise that the laws mandated. Instead, educators used the children's zip codes, their skin color, or their parents' income as a prerequisite to give them adequate appropriate education that enabled lifelong success.

Samuels (2008) confirmed that IEP students faced uphill battles in their respective environments. In the findings, Samuels discovered that the 2005 U.S. Supreme Court's decision in *Schaffer v. Weast* put schools' staff members against parents in its decision. It stipulated that parents had the responsibility of proving the inadequacy of their child's IEP. This put the parents, according to Samuels, in an unfair situation because they are ill equipped with no expert resources at their disposal to fight with resourceful school districts. Knowing this, the districts often challenged the parents to "sue." Some parents accepted the challenge and proceeded while others ended the dispute and remained frustrated. However, in the rare events of a parent prevailing in a lawsuit, the school district is under no obligation to reimburse the parent for expert witness(es).

5

Focus on Success

Support Data

The SED's report card and the eleven districts A through K investigated for this research highlighted some common factors and variables among the districts that showed success or failure. Griffin (1988) indicated that students became the product of the content in which they found themselves. Contingently, if the curriculum was good, the climate healthy, and educators taught well, students learned. Furthermore, schools had students who could operate and produce under such circumstances. Moreover, those students who succeeded perceived school as a problem-solving event. The researcher concluded that there was no good or bad strategy or method to teach, unless it was considered for the specific purposes accomplished.

Billingsley, Carlson, and Klein (2004) also found that working conditions, teacher support, salary, school climate, and job manageability are key factors for success. These researchers in their study "The Working Conditions and Induction Support of Early Career Special Educators" proved that although beginning special education teachers had different categories of disabilities in their classes, insurmountable paperwork, and problems with student behavior and discipline, they tried to succeed in their jobs. More than 50 percent remained at their jobs when the school climate was positive, and the administration and colleagues supported and helped them.

Billingsley (2004) did a further study, "Promoting Teacher Quality and Retention in Special Education," and reported that professional development, emotional and instrumental support, and extensive support by colleagues and administrators allowed for successful results in school districts. Such actions, the reporter claimed, correlated with job satisfaction that in turn transfers to academic success. The reporter also indicated that the greater the levels of administrative support, the greater the job satisfaction and commitment among special educators. The report concluded that school districts and their success were contingent upon the administrators who were in a powerful position to shape the organizational conditions in which teachers worked. They had an impact on many different facets of school life such as school climate, teacher roles, and resources.

The results of the eleven districts A through K noted on the SED's report card and the investigation by the present researcher showed similar factors of the successful districts. Additionally, schools that fostered high self-esteem and promoted social scholastic success had high expectations for all students. They showed compassion, understanding, respect, and interest for children and their families. Similarly, good management, organization, appropriate accommodations, and early intervention programs all generated success (Appalachia Educational Laboratory 1996-2005).

Gates (2005) signified that when schools organized their curriculum to educate the poor and minority, those students develop independence and self-sufficiency. These schools, claimed Gates, organized their curriculum to educate the students around the following principles:

- Ensuring all students received a challenging curriculum that prepared them for college or work.
- Their courses related to their lives and goals when adults in their lives pushed them to achieve; and parents, teachers, and communities worked together to help them attain the same.

Saunders (2005) concurred that the intervention processes that untrained providers delivered resulted in under-education to special-needs children. Eventually, vast numbers of students showed up at school needing a greater number of expensive special education services, which well-trained personnel could have prevented at the beginning of their schooling.

The research also showed that the main building block of the education of special-needs children rested on funding and money. However, adequate funding caused the elimination of many programs that helped them.

According to Nettleton (2004), people with disabilities were people who received a label through diagnosis. The labels determined the process of their education and limited their recognition as human beings.

Nettleton also affirmed that children with disabilities achieved more when teachers saw them as people first and not their disabilities. However, students progressed in spite of their disabilities when treated with dignity, self-respect, and as regular people.

In addition, Hayden (2005) found that a student felt confident and overcame negatives when a teacher or service provider believed in him/her.

Hoff (2007) reiterated that success was guaranteed when schools created learning communities that embraced different learning styles and diversity of all background. As well, reaching out to parents who might be unable to communicate effectively was as viable as the programs in the schools.

The reporter insisted that schools were more successful when federal legislators listened to principals who knew the school population, changed the current laws to ones that required more flexibility and funding, and created more effective and less punitive atmosphere that would affect generations of children.

In support of the previous findings, McGrath (2007) and Supovitz (2007) in separate investigation attested that respecting teachers, giving them clear vision in instructional quality in major content areas, allowed them to use their professional discretion effectively while balancing persuasive and coercive methods to build system-wide commitment to students, districts, and communities.

Carroll (2008) also confirmed findings about the relationship of success of schools and teacher productivity. Carroll found that teachers accelerated their effectiveness if and when their day-to-day work at their school was enhanced by professional development. Teachers also produced exceptionally well when they were provided with a career path that recognized and rewarded their accomplishments, deepening their effectiveness and expertise while supporting, rewarding, and encouraging multiple career paths. Accordingly, reported Carroll, these teachers became engaged in a cultural transformation of their schools and support twenty-first-century teaching and learning.

Learning Style

Nettleton also maintained that it was important to take into consideration the differences in people because a normal school population had students in a regular class with other students that fell between the norm and average ability of progress. However, addressing the needs of exceptional or disabled students' individuality was unique and successful, for disability was only one part of a student (Nettleton

2004). In addition, although some children suffered the same illness, they did not necessarily heal the same way. So, too, disabilities did not affect all children the same way (Equal Rights 1995). Some children used visual aid effectively while others wanted audio aids. As well, a student's learning style determined the uniqueness of his or her IEP. Griffin (1988) emphasized that the special-needs children's differences and ability to succeed depended on the outcome of their experiences in their home, community, and school. A consequence of living in their world depended on what they did or could not do in school. Service providers helped special-needs children when they recognized the unique differences in each child, where a child's personality and style became crucial in addressing his or her special interests (Including the Disabled Student, n.d.; Schwarz 1995; McPherson 2005).

Another report outlined that students achieved more in their own comfortable learning environment. PL 94-142 stipulated "least restrictive environment," which emphasized that successful student progressed in warm, inviting, alternative settings that challenged them and the educators. This held true whether the special-needs children learned effectively or poorly (Billingsley 2004; Appalachia Educational Laboratory 1996-2005).

IEP

The uniqueness in each child determined the design and implementation of his/her tailored program. The program, called an IEP, when followed correctly guaranteed success for the special-needs students in the education process. In some instances, however, LD (learning disabled) students became confused when their teacher did a lecture lesson and the students failed to understand. Ainscow and Tweedle (1979) found that very often children who had difficulty with learning did so because for whatever reason they failed to understand the instructions. And the teacher neglected to realize the crucial difference in language from pupil to pupil (Overton et al. 2004).

Others emphasized that students succeeded when they understood the vocabulary that the teacher used when working with the student. The IEP that the parent, service provider, student, and administration developed had a mastery date and accomplishment level. Mastery level for each student differed, depending on the child's learning style and ability. The experienced teacher devised strategies to address needs and success rate. That teacher using many commonalities between strategy, intervention programs, and direct instruction programs guaranteed success. Combination of these specific components enhanced positive outcomes (Swanson, Hoskyn, Lee, Billingsley et al. 2004; Gates 2005).

Accordingly, Behrmann and Jerome (2002) disclosed the need for a different design and modality for students who were easily distracted. They found that multimedia tools—assistive technology—helped these students tremendously. They specified, for example, that the Internet communication system transported the students beyond their physical environment, allowing them to interact with people far away, and engaged them in interactive learning experiences through CompuPals.

As well, learning-disabled students with reading difficulties enhanced their reading skills by e-mailing and instant messaging with other students. In order to generate more messages, they also developed writing skills and the ability to use the dictionary and the encyclopedia. These learning processes helped the visual and audio learners. Simultaneously, the audio learners had to access their voice mail and vice versa.

As a result, these multimedia tools enhanced teaching, learning, and individual capabilities. The students organized their thoughts or tasks using flow charts, task analysis, e-books, e-mail, instant messaging, voice mail, CompuPals, and other assistive technology to strengthen their skills.

Nonetheless, multimedia tools have helped significantly and hurt much as well as Shaw (2008) revealed. His research indicated that as a consequence, multimedia tools have diminished reading among college students. This resulted in negativity that impacted civic, cultural, economic, and social trends markedly.

Shaw warned of the decline of reading in the United States because TV, computer, texting, video games, and iPods have stolen very crucial skills away from books and reading. The report stressed the growing concern of educational performance today. He advocated for school and home to encourage reading—the basis of the educational process.

Social Interaction

Special-needs children who had a poor opinion of themselves lost confidence and brought an expectation of failure with them into the classroom (Ainscow and Tweedle 1979; Schwarz 1995). Unfortunately, they did not socialize very well. Many factors like poverty, ill health, and hunger contributed to this depression in the students. Nevertheless, the students were encouraged to "get up and go" by the educator who instilled in them that their society taught them to inherit worth instead of a place that determined what they became in life. It also helped with their self-confidence when the student realized that the educator depended on them to make a difference for themselves (Special Education Inclusion, n.d.; McCubbin et al. 1995; Levine and Askins 2004; Steely, n.d.).

Self-confidence promoted self-esteem. According to McCubbin et al. (1998) and Enable Human Rights and Disabled Persons (2003-2004), a human being—every special child—also experienced a physical entity with a unique generic inheritance, in possession of a certain state of physical health and well-being. That human being, according to the researchers, of a particular age, living through a certain developmental stage in his or her life, had a specific history. Inside that human being, memories, ideas, goals, images, feelings, sensations, drives, impulses, and a consciousness developed. Outside the being, a physical world, social and cultural values, assumptions, and ways existed. All these characteristics came into play and helped each individual become a unique person. Planning for a child contained some variables that helped with the planning for each special child who reacted to the world.

To encourage positive social interaction, teachers and parents described a social skill and explained why, when, where, and how to use it appropriately. Then actual demonstration became pertinent in social skills training. Furthermore, parents and teachers needed to provide specific feedback about correct and incorrect performance to ensure full learning (Wallace and McLoughlin 1988; Initiatives 1997; Martin 2003; Appalachia Educations Laboratory 1996-2005).

Build Strength

However, encouraging special-needs students was an ongoing job that required well-trained and flexible teachers (Harte 2004; Steely, n.d.). A good teacher becomes a coach who places his athletes in the position they performed best. Likewise, a teacher builds on the student's strengths and strengthens his weaknesses. A coach's job is to do what's necessary to help the athlete excel to the maximum of his or her potential. The coach challenges his players to find motivation and drives within themselves (Griffin 1998; Martin 2003; Appalachia 2005). Similarly, a special educator does the same as a coach: encourages, motivates, praises, or corrects when necessary. The coach, as the teacher, teaches skills of goal setting, self-analysis, self-correction, and teamwork. The teacher, as the coach, challenges the student to put forth his best. The teacher, like the coach, watches while the students perform. Good performance enhances achievement, and the students become the doer of the plan generated for them. They would receive props and encouragement from the teacher (Staten Island Advance 2003; Hale 2001).

Self-esteem and Character Development

Some researchers indicated that special students needed to base their decision on self-worth or their own internal standards and past levels of attainment rather than success through their own creativity, capabilities, limitations, and idiosyncrasies as learners per their relativity to task. In the meantime, the students visualized where they wanted to go and became flexible and vigilant to change in priorities or circumstances (Martin 2003; Steedman 1997-2001).

Other reports claimed that when educated, students became self-starters, self-watchers, and self-correctors that are more effective. Moreover, they decided what goals were appropriate for them. In order to achieve in school, they engaged in goal-directed thinking. It boosted their ego when they realized that they achieved success and more so if they participated in the planning strategy. A successful student then elected reasonable goals and generated suitable means to accomplish them. It encouraged growth when they accomplished success implementing their own plans. In this way, adaptive education brought positive results where the students mastered the following strategies (Griffin 1998; Including the Disabled Students, n.d.; Shelly, n.d.; McPherson 2005):

- Instruction was based on the assessed abilities of each student.
- Students worked at their own pace.
- Students received periodic reports of their meeting.
- Alternative materials and activities were provided.
- Students helped one and another to achieve individual and group goals.

Yet more researchers found that special education students became confident when they prioritized their goals. These researchers conducted a study to determine the effectiveness and result of modifications of the instruction, the role of the teacher, the participation of the students, the selection of matching students, and a safe environment for teaching and learning. In the study, small groups of special-needs students worked cooperatively with positive feedback by the teachers. The results showed the action and situation facilitated academic learning (79%), engendered active participation in learning (71%), and afforded opportunity for important social learning (71%). In conclusion, the student retained information and talked to each other, but the most cited benefit was self-esteem (Jenkins, Antil, Wayne, and Vadasy 2003).

Another study used the Piers-Harris Children's Self-Concept Scale to evaluate self-esteem among 143 special-needs students. The study reported that medication lowered self-esteem, but positive role models and the mind-set impacted self-worth and self-esteem. Furthermore, sensitivity to a child's culture improved his or her functional level that promoted self-esteem (Bussing, Zima, and Perwien 2000).

Even other researchers indicated that self-monitoring, self-management, and self re-enforcement produced meaningful improvement in student on task behavior, academic productivity, accuracy, and reduction of inappropriate or disruptive behaviors. This study determined the treatment of using multimodal approach on students with attention deficit/hyperactivity disorder (ADHD). Included in the approach were medication, behavior modification, school accommodations, and ancillary services. Self-regulation, as a result, boosted self-esteem (Reid, Trout, and Schartz 2005).

Similarly, Karvonen, Test, Wood, Browder, and Algozzine (2004) also found that self-determination boosted self-esteem where students with disabilities took greater responsibility for their learning. That study analyzed data through a cross-case analysis where they gathered qualitative data to examine stakeholder perceptions of self-determination (SD) outcome of six programs with disabled students. All the teachers and assistants consistently helped the students evaluate their options and anticipated the consequences of their decisions. This helped the students take responsibility for the outcomes of those decisions. In short, students could not blame anyone else for their mistakes or shortcomings.

As the aforementioned researches signified, self-esteem helped students to take responsibility. So, too, character development is crucial in helping the special children set goals. This was evidenced in the study done by the World TEAM Sports (2002). That study signified that through sports, people with disabilities built healthy minds and bodies as they focused on "it's not what happens to you in life, it's how you deal with it." With that slogan imbedded in their minds, the disabled worked together, set goals, competed, achieved, and built interpersonal relationships. They learned through their unique sports activities to give and accept compliments, communicated through writing, and analyze and critique strategies positively. In the end, they developed self-awareness, prompting self-assessment and perseverance. In turn, they set their own goals with great success and overcame all existing stereotyping, thereby building their character.

TEAM Sports complemented the character education that Muscott and O'Brien (1999) highlighted, showing former secretary of education William Bennett as the initiator in 1993 and former president Clinton echoing the movement in 1996 when he declared, "I challenge all our schools to teach character education, to teach good values and good citizenship." The president then set forth three important goals for character education:

— Good character helped all become fully human, more capable of work, and love by building strength of mind, heart, and will.
— Schools were better places when they were civil, and caring human communities that promulgated, taught, celebrated, and held students and staff accountable to the values on which good character was based.
— Teaching character education was essential to the task of building a moral society.

Based on the emergence of character education, Muscott and O'Brien (1999) examined studies done by Patterson, Reid, Jones, and Conger (1975); Quay (1986); and Asher and Hymel (1981) who pointed out that deficits in social skills caused loneliness, problems in maintaining relationships, social isolation, and peer rejection among young people. They then followed up with a study and found that preparation for citizenship required the following six pillars of character development:

— Responsibility and self-control
— Cooperation and teamwork
— Respect and appreciation of diversity
— Trustworthiness
— Fairness and justice
— Caring

They also found that many disabled students lacked character traits such as respect, responsibility, honesty, empathy, tolerance, and cooperation. To develop character education among the students, Muscott and O'Brien 1999 trained mentors to serve as follows:

— Effective caregivers who treated younger students with respect while helping them succeed at all activities
— Moral models who demonstrated a high level of respect and responsibility in their interactions with others, and discussed morally significant events
— Ethical mentors who provided direct instruction and guidance through explanation, storytelling, discussion, encouragement of positive behavior and corrective feedback when students engaged in behavior that was hurtful to themselves or others

The result signified that students with behavioral and other learning disabilities were extremely satisfied with the program they perceived to be about fun, friendship, teamwork, cooperation, and learning.

The researchers interviewed the students who revealed that the program taught them many skills including how to cooperate with students of different ages, to solve problems, the meaning of citizen leader or team member, the responsibility when confronted with the answers to a test, and how to reach out to peers from diverse backgrounds who were new to the school.

Stable Environment

Students with disabilities achieved their potential through adaptive education with a talented, dedicated, and well-prepared teacher in their classroom (Ed Initiatives 1997-08). Nevertheless, Shawinski (2004) emphasized that teaching posed a challenge for teachers who wanted to do an effective and appropriate job for the benefit of the special child. However, despite some research that showed a tremendous attrition and burnout among special education teachers, there were dedicated teachers who helped special students (Billingsley 2004).

Teachers kept their jobs and influenced their students positively when the working environment supported them. Skilled, dedicated teachers gave students with disabilities opportunities that were otherwise inaccessible to them (Shawinski 2004). In addition, Saunders (2005) reaffirmed that uniquely qualified teachers in the classroom helped special children achieve their potential.

Billingsley (2004) stressed the importance of retaining qualified teachers to teach special-needs children. To do this, the researcher indicated that teachers with positive work conditions and appropriate professional development were the catalyst for higher maximum retention of teachers. She emphasized that development must be "ongoing," intensive, and supported by modeling and collective solving of specific problems of practice. The report continued to explain the importance of such developmental workshops, which guaranteed prevention of teacher burnout, heightening teachers' sense of efficacy and improving teachers' practice. Additionally, the report concluded that the retention-enhancing factors also cultivated qualified special educators by providing the conditions where they grew and thrived professionally and holistically. This way the teachers sustained the special educators' commitment to help the special-needs children reach their highest potential.

Contrary to the positive outcomes of a stable school environment, Jacobsen (2005) reported that some teachers and almost one-third of secondary students claimed there was no support in their respective schools. The students affirmed that they did not receive any guidance about what classes to take or information about where some offices or facilities were located.

Teachers also complained that they were lost because they received no formal or informal mentoring from experienced teachers or anyone else. They did not feel positive about their relationships with students, other teachers, or principals.

On the other hand, Nougaret, Scruggs, and Mastropieri (2005), in their study evaluating licensed first-year teachers and teachers with emergency provisional licensure, found that teachers in the traditional education group outperformed first-year teachers with emergency provisional licensure on observational ratings of planning and preparation and classroom environment and instruction. They based their study on the extreme shortage of licensed special education teachers when many school districts implemented emergency licensure at increasing rates. In those instances, the teachers had little or no formal teacher education, which minimized their effectiveness. They concluded that teacher education produced better special education teachers.

Freedom of Choice

As indicated previously, students with disabilities excelled tremendously when they made decisions that boosted their self-esteem (Jenkins et al. 2003). Other researchers showed that choice making by individuals with disabilities proved successful when teachers, parents, and the students expressed confidence in the students. They described the students exhibiting such self-determination as "let people know what they want" and "won't take no for an answer." Their confidence included excitement in their upcoming graduation, negotiating options with their teachers, accepting their disabilities, compensating for it, and attending the local colleges. In addition, parents even spoke about their children's self-advocacy (Karvonen et al. 2005).

An earlier study indicated that special-needs children could not achieve their potential, crucial in boosting self-esteem and creativity, when students became increasingly critical of the ways in which professionals underestimated their abilities and undervalued their wishes that included the following:

- Expressing their thoughts and feelings
- Making choices and decision
- Provided information on their rights

- Allowed to make changes in their own lifestyles

This became an important factor because each student had a unique IEP and wanted treatment as individuals (Tilstone 1998; Enable 2003-04).

Unique Needs and Instruction

Because each disabled student required a special tailored program, schools and teachers demonstrated flexibility to handle that demand (Including the Disabled Student, n.d.). However, a previous study by Greene (1986) showed that some of these students had instruction modeled to them. Nevertheless, they could not grasp the concept because it was not relevant or related to any of their experiences. He warned that measuring a child's ability by predicting his or her potential was not valid. He explained that certain factors and variables became expedient in considering each child's manner: "Genetics + genetics environment + psychological factor + potential ability, and potential ability + desire + effort + developed ability" simply meant, a special-needs child must have the desire to be motivated to exert effort in order to achieve success, which depended on the child's genetics, environment, and psychological factors. Greene demonstrated in the following exchange between a student, Erik, and an interrogator. Erik, a student in a private high school, also had a private tutor for eleven years and accepted the fact that he needed to work harder.

Erik's skills: one year below grade level. After counseling, Erik agreed to a tailored program, emphasizing academic and study skills. He progressed very well as a student. He decided to go to a four-year college. His grades and attitude deteriorated when the counselor recommended that Erik not do higher-level studies after receiving Cs in Algebra 11 and chemistry. Erik became outraged and engaged in the following dialogue:

> Erik: It all seems worthless now. All that work. The counselor has made up his mind that I am not college material. What right does he have to tell me what I can do and cannot do? How does he know how smart I am, or how hard I am willing to work? I have made progress. For the first time I am getting decent grades. The only reason I got a C in both courses is the work I did at the beginning of the semester. My recent grades in quizzes and tests were much better. I got a C on the Algebra final and a C+ on the biology final.

The tutoring is helping. I am finally beginning to understand Algebra. The study skills class taught me how to study for the biology tests.

Interrogator: Then you feel the counselor is being unfair?

Erik: Yes! I am going to fight! I got authorization from the teachers. Now he is saying that is not good enough. It's as if the counselor doesn't believe that I can do it.

Erik's persistence and determination permitted him to enter the higher-level courses. In spite of his learning difficulties and the barriers erected by the counselor, Erik passed the advanced courses. He received B in each class. By basing his assessment of Erik's potential ability exclusively on his past record, the counselor neglected to consider Erik's personality. The researcher concluded that Erik learned efficiently because he possessed the ability to concentrate, to remember, to think analytically, to decipher written and spoken language, to understand how numbers worked, and to express concrete and abstract ideas (Greene 1988, 50).

Greene indicated that the teachers, not the counselor, knew Erik's capabilities. They trusted and encouraged him, and he excelled. That gave him an opportunity to move to a higher level. The counselor recommended against it, disappointing Erik tremendously.

CASE STUDIES

As indicated, the researcher for this paper also uncovered several disparities among funding (Truscott et al. 2004), implementing laws (Olsen 2000), qualified teachers (Billingsley 2004), disproportionate number of minority students targeted for special-needs students (Hosp and Reschly 2004), and the lack of funding to help these disadvantaged children. Overwhelming evidence showed that special-needs children succeeded when educators gave them a chance to succeed (Sinclair et al. 2005; Reid et al. 2005). The researcher for this paper also observed five special students from the beginning of their high school to the end of their high school years. The results are as follows:

Case no. 1: Connie was a very attractive, very popular girl with long thick black hair. She had a very clear legible handwriting. She became the manager of the track team in her junior year in high school. She neglected to complete her homework or to answer question in class and fought with the teacher constantly. The fights escalated to the point where Connie rushed to the main office to complain. The teacher could not understand. The teacher was firm and refused to accept anything less than their best. She insisted on her class rules on assignments. She graded and logged every grade. Connie came to a realization that she had to show some work. The teacher in a careers skills class asked all the juniors, including Connie, to fill out applications for jobs. Connie was the only one who did not turn in one. She gave numerous excuses. The teacher refused to accept the excuses because it was a class activity. She insisted. She asked another student to bring an application from a particular business and gave Connie to fill out. Connie did. The next part of the activity was to submit the application to the respective business. Some 90% of the students acquired a job. The applications were to the local supermarkets, banks, deli, pastry shops, convenience stores, fast food restaurants, and other local businesses. When it was Connie's turn, she was terrified. She continued her excuses.

Eventually, Connie realized that she could not avoid the activity. She waited and watched for the teacher. When the class was empty, Connie grasped the opportunity and explained to the teacher that she wanted help to count money. She had never gone to the store because her father shopped for everything. He had his three children, especially the two girls and the mother, very sheltered. Supermarket problems, bank activity, and shopping became an ongoing activity for Connie and her class. Connie became confident by the time she entered the twelfth grade because other avenues were opening up to her. She focused more and was able to complete homework assignments.

Connie bravely went out with one of her classmates to apply for a job. A company hired her as a telemarketer for minimum wage, three days per week. She was able to branch off to a more stable job soon after to the great displeasure of her father. Unfortunately, her father died of a heart attack one day while Connie was at school. Connie was devastated. She later graduated on time. That teacher wrote a letter to a higher education institution, describing Connie's strengths and weaknesses. She was accepted. And with the help of the people at that institution, Connie maintained a 3.5 GPA. She graduated and now is the breadwinner of the family. She owns a car and takes care of her mom and sister.

Case no. 2: Dan, a special education student, could not read. Nevertheless, he was cooperative and had good interpersonal skills. He never received any pressure to pass a Regents exam, and he did not drop out. However, he was skilled with his hands. In school, he had very clean notebooks and copied notes neatly though he could not read them. He respected authority and was never absent from classes from ninth through twelfth grades. He became the teacher's helper in many instances. At the end of his twelfth grade, he realized that he must be out of there as a young adult. A job was on his mind because of his very good references describing his capabilities, from his teachers. A major hospital hired him to do janitorial work. After two years, he became a manager until the present time. He also acquired a driver's license.

Case no. 3: Noel is another special-needs student who liked to eat. He knew how to read, but he could not stay still in his seat. He told his teacher that he wanted to know how to cook. He did not do any Regents exam because it was optional. At the end of his senior year, the guidance counselor helped him to fill out an application to attend a cooking school. The school accepted him, and now he works in a restaurant.

Case no. 4: Shelly, a beautiful tall special-needs student never believed that she would work hard. She had her mind set on becoming a fashion model and dressed inappropriately for school. In the meantime, the school enrolled her in the BOCES health skills program. She completed the twelfth grade and proceeded to follow her dream. Fortunately, she disbanded the modeling program. She is a hospital employee with her own apartment and raising her son as a single mother.

Case 5: Benny, a Spanish immigrant, depended on his manliness and handsomeness to get through school. In the ninth through eleventh grade, Benny looked for the beautiful girls. He was very street-smart but could not read. He was a good dresser who often took vacations from school to travel. At the end of his eleventh grade, Benny realized that he must do something with his life. He approached his teacher and investigated possibilities of obtaining a job in the field he liked. The teacher outlined the skills and requirements. In the ninth through eleventh grade, Benny worked inconsistently in class, spent a great part of the day in the hallways, was very street-smart, but could not read. Benny took vacation while school was in session to travel. At the end of the eleventh grade, Benny realized the error of his ways and decided to get his priorities straight. He was determined to change and make something of his life. He sought help, improved his academic skills, and attended BOCES to pursue auto mechanic skills. Benny graduated. Now he has a full-time job working as an auto mechanic assistant.

Discussion

The foregoing researchers emphasized that children succeeded if they were determined, saw relevance to their needs, and had the opportunity to make decisions pertinent to their goals and achievements. However, the state mandates, including the NCLB Act and the HOPE scholarship, force the special-needs students to do tests that humiliate them and deem them failures.

6

Anecdotal Studies

Observation and Interviews

The investigator continued to collect information from schools other than A through K, the primary research project. The opportunity presented itself when the researcher was one of the three educators sent to observe certain new programs in other schools. The following represented the researcher's interviews and observations of five schools.

Five Different Schools

School no. 1. The SED report card identified this high school as in the 95-99% range receiving Regents diploma, with more than 1,500 students in enrollment and a similar profile to C in figures 1 and 2. The researcher followed a special education class for one day with the intent of uncovering their secret of success. The facts are as follows:

- Before the bell signaling the beginning of school, all the students hung out in the schoolyard and parking lot, smoking, playing music, joking, eating, screaming, and socializing.
- About 85% of the students owned a car.
- Some of them wore very colorful hair; both male and female wore loud or dark clothing.
    - They ignored strangers in their parking lot or schoolyard.

- At the sound of the bell, they discarded the food and smokes and proceeded immediately to class.
- Two minutes after the bell, the halls were completely clear of students, except for new or lost students.
- Security personnel in regular clothes gave directions as needed.
- Students remained engaged and focused on the task(s).
- Special students were included in the regular classes.
- In each inclusion situation, there were at least four teachers in the classroom.
- The special students then went on to enrichment or skills class to enhance the skills learned in the inclusion class.
- Special education students participated, asked questions, gave suggestions, and worked along with the regular education peers with pride.

The special students were responsible for the same assignments, whether it was to read five chapters, write a critical lens essay, research an item, make a flowchart, solve challenging math problems, or create a business proposal.

The support system for the special students was incredible. The adults worked with each student on a one-to-one basis to yield the required results.

Every special student wrote for all Regents examinations.

The researcher then investigated the factors that helped generate such success in the school. The liaison of the special education and general education programs responded.

The liaison attributed the success to the collegiality among the staff who volunteered to work in the program. The teachers had meetings after school, before school, and in between. They used the curriculum to plan lessons for their students who were motivated and eager to learn more. The students also challenged the teachers, who must be better prepared with updated facts to provide answers to students who sought help. The students also used their time away from school to do research on many different topics. They did not work in any job outside the home or school. In addition, if a student, special or regular, did not produce as well as the standards set for him or her, the liaison called the parent immediately and set up an appointment for a visit. Either the parent must come to the school or the school would go to the home.

The liaison gave an example of a special education student who did not return homework assignment to class. When asked the reason for the homework violation, the student responded that there was too much noise in his house so he could not concentrate. The school visited the home and discussed the matter with the parent, who agreed to provide a better home-study environment for the student by signing a good faith contract, fulfilling her parental duties. The school followed up with encouragement until there was significant improvement on both sides—parent and child.

The liaison emphasized that another factor that helped the success of the special students was the involvement of the community and added that the school sent out newsletters regularly to the community about the issues, problems, rewards, and projects of the school. She stressed that the people in the community did not tolerate anything less than perfect in the school system. The people, therefore, kept up with the progress of each child and claimed that they expected top dollars for their homes, so the school had an obligation to deliver. In one instance in that particular school, the researcher observed a well-dressed woman in her late fifties working in the skills classroom with two other adults and three special education students. The woman had left her job in management on Wall Street, where she earned a substantial salary. The woman proclaimed that the school needed her more than the job. She also indicated that some students needed help, and she was willing to help put her district on the top of the SED's list.

The researcher observed all students working in a cooperative manner with the adults. The teachers present treated all students equally although there were no minority students or teachers present. The special students were not identifiable in the classroom, and the teacher assistants made sure that the students copied the homework assignment or board notes correctly. It was a team effort that generated absolute success.

School no. 2. This school portrayed similar factors and results. It was a middle school with a similar economics status and profile as District H. The researcher spent a 40-minute period in an eight-grade special education social studies class, which compromised of 17 students, 3 teachers aides, and 2 teachers. In this class, the teachers and students used the homeland security idea of color codes as a behavior plan for the students. Students in this class were 100% white, with 69.1% male and 30.8% female. They all took their learning very seriously. In their skills period class the special students brought all their academic problems for help. Upon entering the classroom, the researcher could not tell that it was an inclusion class because all the students worked on the same level. The special educators and aides worked with all the students.

School no. 3. Then the researcher visited a school that has less than 50% success rate on the SED's report card, similar to District G. The supervisor for the special education department escorted the researcher to her office for a meeting. The supervisor expressed dissatisfaction with the report card classification of this school. She articulated frustration over being treated "like step children" by the district administrator. When questioned about the factors that contributed to the low grades of the district, and more so, the special education students, she complained that the lack of resources was affecting the department negatively. She outlined the many requests that the district had put on hold. She indicated that in order to help boost her special students' progress, she wanted and asked for the following:

- A chairperson to coordinate and supervise the program in each school
- Aides or teacher assistants to work with each of the five special education teachers and to follow the state mandate
- The servicing of students according to their IEPs
- Permanent rooms where the special education student would feel comfortable
- More special education teachers to service the more than seventy-five students in the high school
- Mentor programs for beginning teachers

All she received from the district was "You have to wait. The district is trying its best, but we have a more lucrative situation to work on."

This left the special education students to survive the best way possible under the circumstances. Each of the five special education teachers worked with inappropriately assessed children. When asked about the state mandates compliance and the community response, the supervisor indicated that she did only what the superiors allowed.

The supervisor also reported that the special students were cognizant of their labels because at times while acting out, defying authority, or engaging other students negatively, they would indicate that their labels protected them from all punishment.

The observation revealed that this school had certified veteran special education teachers who guaranteed their dedication and willingness to do their utmost for the special students. But they expressed their frustration in the regular educators denying them their equal rights. They claimed that the regular education department did not acknowledge them as qualified educators. They also indicated that the regular educators did not share willingly any information with them, the special educators. When a child acted negatively in the halls or any public arena, the regular educator oftentimes humiliated the special educator by suggesting that the student belonged to the special education department.

In addition, the school had a 90% minority enrollment with 95% of the teachers in the building being white. The students were loud in the halls even after the bell signified the beginning of the school day. Security guards patrolled the building continuously.

School no. 4. This school where the success level on the SED's report card was less than 30% has an enrollment of close to 2,000 students in this two-storey building. Here the special education students occupied the back of the school with access doors leading to the street. The enrollment is 100% minority students with 75% of the staff white and middle class. This school has a similar profile to District A.

The special students displayed a range of behavior in this junior high school. They picked on each other throughout the class session and tried to gain attention through negative behavior. This special class had fifteen students, one certified special teacher, and one paraprofessional without even a high school diploma. The paraprofessional controlled the kids who gave the most trouble. The teacher organized the class in groups with matching or compatible students. They played different games. The teacher explained that the students could not read but they liked to rap, liked to tell dirty jokes, and were very streetwise. When questioned about special education rules, regulations, and the NCLB Act and compliance, the teacher agreed that the school was noncompliant.

The special education teacher also disseminated some pertinent information to the researcher. She declared that the parents did not show up for parent/teacher conferences, the students were not motivated, and teachers worked accordingly. She also expressed regret for not being able to help the students in her charge and concluded that most of the special students dropped out before going into high school.

School no 5. The fifth school for the researcher's observation and interviews proved to be very interesting. This high school scored 50% on the SED's report. The investigator found that most of the special education teachers were moving from location to location with their school supplies and materials on a rolling cart. The special education department included four teachers with sixty-five students among them. In a meeting with them, the researcher corroborated a lot of evidence from the ongoing studies. The teachers claimed that other subject area teachers had priority for classroom space, and they lamented that they always received required services after every other teacher did. Consequently, they had classrooms in a closet, a bathroom, or some small space with inadequate ventilation, no closet space for personal belongings, and no shelves or cabinets for books or materials.

One veteran teacher also described a situation where the high school expected more students from the feeder school than there was classroom space. To accommodate the new classes, the administrators moved the special education teacher from a room in favor of a regular education class. The displaced special education teacher had to wait four weeks for a classroom that was smaller, brightly colored, no chalkboard or bulletin board, and inadequate ventilation. The teacher protested but to no avail.

Discussion

The foregoing interviews and observations highlighted issues and problems corroborating the prior researchers' report on the special education dilemma. The evidence uncovered so far showed that failure or success in any one district does not necessarily contribute to failure or success in another district. For instance, the researcher examined the factors in the following illustrations:

Edy and her family migrated to the United States from South America when she was seven years old so they might have a better quality of life. The oldest of three children, Edy attended elementary, middle, and high schools in District G. Although shy, even as a learning-disabled nonreader in a special education class, Edy made friends with her classmates and became more outgoing. By the eleventh grade, Edy dressed only in black outfits with black mascara circles around the eyes, spikes around the neck, black lipstick, tattoos, nose rings, and armbands and became uncooperative and disinterested in academics. According to her IEP, Edy had no decoding skills and could not do math. During the second quarter of the eleventh grade, Edy's family moved to a different neighborhood—District B—where she made new and different friends. Her new school scored 90% and above in graduation and college enrollment level on the SED's report card.

Ultimately, Edy graduated early, fifteen months later, from the new high school and enrolled in college where she pursued a career in criminal justice. She no longer dressed in black outfits, black eyeliner, studs, nose rings, armbands, and colorful hair. She is now very articulate and a self-assured young woman.

Kino is a five feet ten black male who also grew up in District G where he attended pre-K, kindergarten, and elementary schools up to the eleventh grade. Kino's classification was learning disabled and a nonreader who required a scribe, questions read, extended time, and many other testing accommodations. Kino attended class late each day because he loitered in the hallways. He slept during class, outtalked the teacher, showed no interest in essay writing, and refused to tackle any math problems.

Upon completion of the eleventh grade, Kino's family moved to a new neighborhood similar to District J, which had a 75% to 85% success rate on the SED's report card. Kino registered and attended the neighborhood school where he spent the first two and a half quarters of his senior year. He attended classes on time, was alert, took notes, and participated in class.

During the third quarter of the school year, situations and circumstances caused Kino's family to relocate back to the old neighborhood where they moved in with family members. Kino returned to his old school, and much to the surprise of the school staff, he was no longer classified as learning disabled; he became a part of regular classes, which he attended on time. He walked with purpose and gusto as he made his way to his classes. He participated in class, read, wrote for himself, and graduated at the end of the school year.

These two comparisons were not enough to affect or cause any changes in the laws or acts enacted. Nevertheless, the question was what caused Edy and Kino to make such a drastic change in such a short time. It takes a long time for children to learn to read and comprehend. Edy, a chronic nonreader with no decoding skills, has undertaken career in criminal justice in a school that required SAT scores and prequalifying examinations.

Did these students have the drive or desire in them that no one tapped into? Did maturity play a part here? Could the environment have influenced the two students to produce or not? Should there be additional study to uncover the variables and dynamics that matter accordingly?

7

INEFFECTIVE STRATEGIES

STATE MANDATES

Pressure on Schools

Conversely, schools that did not have all the factors for success in place failed students. One report indicated that academic failure began in elementary school and, with prolonged and chronic failure, demoralized children, which caused loss of status and rejection by peers, destroyed self-esteem, and undermined feelings of competence. For such students, school was not a place of attachment and learning but of alienation and failure (Appalachia Educational Laboratory 1996-2005).

Schwarz (1995) found that students failed when the teachers and the learners had a mismatched style of learning resulting from limited previous educational experience by the learners whose test scores were flawed. They had problems with intonation, and there were external problems such as health or family crises.

Earlier studies showed that for the special-needs students, the great emphasis placed on increased levels of academic achievement in schools put many of them in a difficult situation where they did not get an opportunity to learn what they needed (Griffin 1988). Wallace and McLoughlin (1988) also affirmed that mainstreaming increased the number of resources and consultant programs in public schools where there were varying state regulations and differential professional training programs.

To meet the new mandates that put tremendous pressure on students to achieve the very high standards set, Davis (2004) contended that states and districts nationwide did everything in their power to obtain state or federal funds. He emphasized that tests scores set the pace or agenda for state and federal aid. In doing so, states were forced to include special students to fulfill the No Child Left Behind Act of 2001. He recommended stronger partnership between general education and special education.

ATTITUDE TOWARD SPECIAL EDUCATION

Community/State

Researchers found that the many problems and issues—including added pressure to secure state and federal aid—provoked varying attitude toward special education on the part of implementers of the enacted rules and regulations.

Goodman and Mann (1976) indicated that scholastic failure resulted from the unwillingness of professionals who worked with special children and were not sensitive to their needs. The professionals, instead of addressing the needs of the specials, enrolled them in remedial classes. The students then, in turn, had lower self-concepts of themselves because the professionals labeled them as children with problems.

Andreatt (2004) stressed that overcrowding damaged the creative activity of students who found themselves in those schools. He claimed that in such schools, students faced many issues:

- Fending for their lives daily
- Using more time thinking about their safety rather than the mechanics of individual subjects
- Devising methods as to how to survive with little or no injury

In his description of the overcrowding schools, Andreatt explained that during the changing of class, the packed hallways incited fights where people got hurt, punched, knocked down, pushed into walls, poked in the eye, and sometimes fell to the floor screaming in pain. He concluded that students and teachers alike spent quality time securing their safety instead of improving the ability of accomplishing the task of taking notes, participating in class activities, extracting significant information out of books, conceptualizing and writing papers, and budgeting time to meet the demands of the schools' curriculum.

A prior study done by Griffin (1988) submitted more evidence of the attitude toward students with unique or special needs. The study showed that students from low-status backgrounds did less well on cognitive relationship among social class, grades, and task assignment, where the low-status students tended to get poorer grades. As well, there was less representation in the academic or college-bound track. In addition, the study claimed that the home environment, even more than the school, explained educational success. Consequently, disadvantaged children entered school without a number of the intellectual skills and aptitudes that most advantaged children possessed. As a result, the disadvantaged students not only lack the wherewithal to achieve success in school, but they also lacked the desire to succeed. These students, in contrast to the advantaged students, usually had difficulty making themselves understood or appearing impressive. The school then spent considerable time trying to accommodate the "natural ways" of these students instead of providing the necessary challenge and opportunity to develop their ability to succeed (IDEA 2004). The children felt their self-worth threatened in the classroom (Schwarz 1995).

Administration

According to McPherson (2005), threatening someone's freedom is a criminal act. Therefore, students whose self-worth and freedom were threatened were also grossly neglected by administrators and school officials. Billingsley (2004) in the research "Promoting Teacher Quality and Retention in Special Education" pointed out factors that produced negative results for special learners. The research looked at the shortage of special educators, the high numbers of uncertified teachers, and high attrition rates and the impact on the education that students with disabilities received.

The report (Billingsley) also noted that administrators were the most important factor in achieving success among special students. They helped improve the students' learning by helping teachers succeed in their job. To accomplish this, administrators who had knowledge about the unique needs of students with disabilities facilitated their staff and students to success. However, the report continued—by citing Crockett (2002)—that many building level administrators who were directly responsible for supervising special education often had limited or no knowledge about special education. Others did not incorporate best practices such as engaging teachers in the learning process or allowing time for them to plan how to implement new skills because they felt that there were many opportunities to learn new techniques and strategies in their district (Morvant et al. 1995, cited by Billingsley 2004). Furthermore, Billingsley signified that administrators played a crucial role in the education of the special students.

The effective and appropriate teaching of the special students hinged on the administrators' attitude in establishing local policies, regulating Individuals with Disabilities Education Act (IDEA), and determining how the services are implemented in their respective districts. However, Robelen (2004) reported that the No Child Left Behind Act did not fulfill its promises to provide schools with resources they needed to educate these students. The lack of resources stemming from these broken promises, according to the "report," undermined the effort of schools to comply with the law and crippled efforts through its ineffective implementation. Truscott et al. (2004), who added some districts overlooked and/or failed to report special education improvements, corroborated this report.

Teacher/School

The teachers became demoralized when the districts and schools overlooked or failed to recognize progress of the special students. As Billingsley (2004) observed, teachers tried to make a difference because they had the most significant role to play in the education of special-needs children. Most beginning special educators began their career with a great deal of optimism, eagerly anticipating the first day of school. However, those eager teachers left when they discovered that their position was an experience of shock and survival. They blamed the experience on their unrealistic expectations in conflict with how to apply what they learned in their preparation programs, the desire to be viewed as competent, and the reluctance to seek help (Billingsley 2004).

Additionally, the reporter expressed that the teachers faced inadequate support and competing responsibilities where their workday was a frustrating experience, without a good job, reasonable workloads, as well as trained mentors. As well, teachers realized ambiguous roles where they shifted from special education classroom instruction to collaborative roles as coteachers and inclusion specialists in general education classes. The new special education teachers had to adjust and change roles depending on the personalities and preferences of the general educators as well as the needs of the students served. The teachers had few opportunities to plan with their coteachers, little training, and many content areas to cover as well. As a result, they felt stressed, overburdened, and unsupported. They had little energy for new learning, supporting others, or trying new approaches to teaching. This led to disillusionment, burnout, and, finally, attrition (Billingsley 2004).

This extensive research indicated that teacher attrition was a major contributor to teacher shortage in special education. Because of the shortage, districts hired many uncertified teachers to work with disabled students. Furthermore, U.S. Department of Education revealed that a great percentage of special education teachers lacked the appropriate special education certification. Other factors complicated the effectiveness of appropriate education to the special children, according to the reports. The special children lost critical learning opportunities as their new uncertified teacher struggled to figure out what to do with the following:

- Limited access to necessary materials
- Difficulty in managing their jobs
- Paperwork that interfered with teaching
- Feelings of not being included in their schools
- Principals who did not support them

From the survey done with beginning special educators, the researchers found that 14.0% of them wanted to remain until retirement, 37.0% wanted to remain as long as they could, 14.0% wanted to remain until something else came around, 7.8% wanted to leave as soon as possible, and 27.0% were undecided (Billingsley 2004; Billingsley et al. 2004).

Also, teachers did not feel comfortable at their jobs, could not, or would not be effective with their students when they, according to Mc Grath, had to perform regularly as security personnel, counselors, police officers, and teachers. Consequently, the students suffered academically.

Many other factors culminated in schools producing failures. Rabb (2007) pointed out that assessment and accountability contributed tremendously to failure where teachers and students ended up bored and frustrated over the following:

- Teachers could not convey their individual passions and interest to their students.
- The practice yielded nothing significant about understanding subject matter among students, but instead
- Gave all illusion of success to everyone in the system but the students, creating an atmosphere of dishonesty, mistrust, and failure among teachers who had taken their jobs seriously. Shaw (2008) also found that many teachers became highly stressed when administrators forced them to focus mainly on test-centered curriculum.

Although advocates realized a need for change in the system to generate more success in schools, the president (Bush) had deprived the states and schools of the resources they needed. On the other hand, test scores became a viable tool to show accountability, which Hoff (2008) disputed as only one facet of success.

Stiggins (2007) cautioned about the consequences of layers of assessment procedures, which produced more failures than they improved learning. This action, the report revealed, cost much time and money and only generated the following myths:

— The path to school improvement is paved with standardized tests.
— School and community leaders know how to use assessment to improve schools.
— Teachers are trained to assess productively.
— Adult decisions drive school effectiveness.
— Grades and test scores maximize student motivation and learning.

Stiggins also asserted that schools that used these myths as guidelines failed their students miserably. Other report showed that failure was a sure result from schools that connected learning to architecture. Kolderie (2008) observed that schools that followed the traditional model devoid of new and different approaches to learning failed the students of this new era because kids don't learn from structure but from what they see, hear, and do.

Dropout

The numerous researchers reflected on the issues and problems including socioeconomics, overcrowding, overrepresentation of minorities, incompetent uncertified teachers, teacher attrition, lack of support, and ambiguous laws that allowed for the lower success rates among special students in some districts.

They also confirmed earlier reports, which stated that educational research oftentimes reflected conflicted aims where the researchers believed in the illusion that failed special students. Hirsh (1996) concluded that inadequate ideas perpetrated educational failure since the 1930s. The history of American determination had been this stubborn persistence of illusion in the face of reality, which resulted in educational decline. Such actions led to disruptive behavior among special children (Appalachia Educational Laboratory 1996-2005; Sinclair 2005).

Another early researcher asserted that disadvantaged students were the losers in the educational decline where the students "lashed out" in an effort to get themselves heard. The report explained that forced bussing, mandated by public schools, created more problems than it solved. The forced bussing meant to provide access to educational opportunity, caused stress, and problems of self-esteem for the children who eventually dropped out. As well, some parents exhibited major concern over whether the disadvantaged children were absorbing a disproportionate amount of the conscientious teacher's time to the neglect of the other children. Conflicts arose resulting in the disadvantaged students resisting school and the advantaged students going to private school (Packard 1983).

As previously discussed, Viadero (2008) described the callousness among school personnel who allowed significant numbers of minority students to roam the halls unimpeded while their white counterparts remained. These students left their classrooms because they felt that the teachers were excluding them subtly by putting them in very uncomfortable situations in the rooms.

In other instances, investigation showed that teacher dropout rate exceeded that of the students mostly in schools where low-income students of color attended. Carroll apprised that the teachers were not given the support they needed to succeed. According to the researcher, these teachers felt the atmosphere did not yield collaboration or communication among colleagues, students, parents, and principals. And that the inferior quality of education delivered to the students rested solely where the students lived.

SURR

Schools where there are many students with poor academic skills and a great percentage of dropouts allowed for poor standing on the education progress ladder of success. Such schools ended up as schools under registration and review (SURR). The students produced very little academically. Research for this paper observed many of these students in some of the districts with similar population, demographic, and socioeconomic status. Of the eleven districts, A through K, investigated, two of them, A and I, became SURR (NYC and NY State Schools District, n.d.).

As is depicted in figure 1, the higher the poverty rates and class size, the lower the graduation rate, enrollment in college, and Regents diploma rates. Achieving SURR status is not a compliment for any school or district. It sends a message telling the public that the schools received poor test results for three consecutive years (SURR press release). Schools listed as SURR need base essentials such as funding, resources, experienced personnel, and committed staff. In order to receive the minimum essentials for achievement, the schools must perform well on standardized tests as well as improve academic status (Olsen 2005). The schools get little funding because of their low test scores. They therefore remain under the scrutiny of all—parents, community, students, administrators, and the state education department. Working conditions and teacher morale become poor, resulting in teacher burnout and attrition (Billingsley et al. 2004).

Through observations and interviews, this researcher uncovered interesting information. During an interview, 80% of the teachers of the SURR contended that they were working at the respective locations because of the following:

— They did minimum work.
— Their commute was short and inexpensive.
— The schools' population was 90% low functioning, requiring little constructive instructional planning.
— There was low staff morale because students were not interested in academics.
— The state department, school principals, and supervisors cared little about compliance.
— Parents never attended parent/teacher conferences or school functions.

Other researchers indicated that in the 2006-2007 school year, many states were overwhelmed by the great number of schools needing improvement. However, McNeil (2008) claimed that state education agencies were struggling with staff turnover, inadequate technology, and insufficient expertise to deal with English language learners. Most of the states deemed the funding of these schools a "constraint," putting the programs and the students at a great disadvantage.

Although one of the goals of NCLB was to help schools with persistently achievement level to improve, Hoff (2008) found that such goals have not been achieved. Instead, Hoff claimed that children with disabilities, racial and ethnic groups, as well as students from low-income families have not improved. In fact, the NCLB used a one-size-fits-all approach as the intervention process for every child. That approach simply could not and did not work, leaving the students and parents in substandard schools. Furthermore, suburban schools using similar methods have not done any better serving poor and minority kids.

8

NCLB's Contradictory Message

Left Behind

African Americans

Despite the ambitious motive of the NCLB Act African-American (black) students have neem consistently left behimd the educational process. In *Learning While Black*, Hale (2001) categorized the victimization of black students across all class barriers as a form of "educational malpractice".

Hale's intensive research demonstrated that "leave no child behind" was a double speak that guaranteed the opposite outcome for black children by uncovering the following facts:

Educational expectations for black boys and girls were generally lower across all social and economic backgrounds.

- Segregated education provided for the majority of African-American students was inferior to that provided for white students.
- In mixed student population, a tracking system in place assigned a disproportionate number of black students to the lower skilled and special education classes and their white counterparts to higher skilled and gifted programs.
- Teachers and psychologists usually took African-American children off the pathway to success, pushing them through the cracks to criminal behavior,

- Parents of these children often lacked the resources to supplement school voucher, or wherewithal to negotiate effective parent conferences with teachers and other professionals.
- The parents also lacked the education, time, or energy to warrant any type of acknowledgement by school officials.

Consequently, black students lag behind a year after year as issues remain buried; and aberrant behaviors become ingrained deep and wide in their souls.

Disadvantaged/Poor/Women

According to Davis (2004), the No Child Left Behind Act (NCLB) of 2001 outlined laws for educators and lawmakers to follow. However, Olsen claimed that the NCLB neglected its promise to fund and help all students, especially the disabled, and this has left many disabled students without appropriate education, leading them to be dependent for life.

Numerous studies concurred with Olsen. Their reports showed that lack of funding and resources allowed the elimination of needed programs for the disabled (Woolfolk 1998; Public Laws regarding Special Education, n.d.). And schools whose students performed in the highest levels of the goals set by the states and the No Child Left Behind Act obtained most of the funding (Rose 2005). There is supporting evidence indicating that the higher the socioeconomic status of the school district, the higher the success rate relevant to the NCLB guidelines (Paglin 2004; Griffin 1988; Paul et al. 1977; Seltzer 1997-2000; Brooks 2001).

From the SED's report card grades, low socioeconomic areas yielded low scores. A scrutiny of the areas as depicted in figures 1 and 2 corroborated the study done by Andreatt (2004) and Paglin (2004), which showed that minority students resided there. Many of the schools in such areas received the uncertified, dissatisfied, frustrated, and burnt-out teachers. In these schools, there was no cooperation, collegiality, and communication among staff members and administration, resulting in attrition among special education teachers (Goodman and Mann 1976; Davis 2004; Billingsley et al. 2004; Billingsley 2004). Moreover, the lack of continuity of resources, accountability, and funding impacted the disadvantaged students very negatively. According to Hosp (2004), the most affected, therefore, were the students who were assessed as special education students and "became a disproportionate number of minority students" and culturally different students (Overton et al. 2004). As a result, the students who needed all the support, resources, and intervention the most did not receive the minimum required skills.

They became disillusioned, scarred, ashamed, and eventually dropped out (Robelen 2004). Other reports reiterated that African American children received a lower quality of education than most white American children did (Hilderbrand 2005; Hosp and Reschly 2004; Schwarz 1995; Hale 2001).

The SED classified these school districts as high poverty areas. The report card profiles depicted in figures 1 and 2 show that the higher the poverty levels, the lower the success rate. The schools in this category then came under review by SURR. Usually, these minority students never had the opportunity to demonstrate any skill and eventually gave up (Packard 1983; Appalachia Educational Laboratory 1996-2005). The parents as well as the students could not earn enough in salaries to make a difference (McCubbin et al. 1997; Wallace and McLoughlin 1988; Steely n.d.; Enable 2003-04; Lynch 2004). SURR students therefore could not access any state or federal funds. Ultimately, the schools in the high socioeconomic levels achieved available resources. The students who needed the funds the most could not acquire the necessary requirements. The ones who needed it the least meet the qualifications with ease and continued to build up more funds (Steedman 1997-2001; Weselthier and Allen 2005; Steely, n.d.).

As the foregoing research pointed out, poor or flawed assessment and testing procedures inappropriately labeled many disadvantaged students. In order to cope with the stigma, some of these students felt defeated with crushed self-esteem and dropped out before the age of seventeen.

Most disadvantaged students, especially the minorities, were poor as demonstrated by Hilderbrand on the report card. Lynch (2004-2005) described poor children as often having inadequate food, safety, shelter, and health care. The report stressed that poor children often fell short of achieving their academic potential, making them more likely to enter adulthood with inadequate skills to compete in today's labor market or to survive independently. Some of these students lash out because of frustration. They believed that they did not get a chance to learn what they needed. They categorized their schools as "dumping grounds for rejects and misfits" that undereducated them. Another report signified that the educationally disadvantaged were also economically disadvantaged who scored less than their "advantaged" counterpart on proficiency exams. More often than not, these students as well could not access federal and state funds.

Not only the mentally, physically, learning, or economically disadvantaged in the aforementioned studies are left behind but other groups as well. Among them are adolescent girls who are usually afflicted with the added disabilities such as dyscalculia, dyslexia, dysgraphia, dysphasia, auditory processing learning disability, attention deficit disorder, social perceptual learning disability, and perceptual motor disability. According to a report cited in *Living Out Loud: Disability*, these girls are prone to numerous problems such as depression (Bodingar-de Uriarte and Austin 1991), drug abuse (Moore 1992), physical and sexual abuse and neglect (Cross, Kaye, and Ratnofsky 1993), teenage pregnancy, and poor academic achievement (Wagner 1992). *Living Out Loud* found that 47% of these girls were African American, and 31%, Latina.

The investigation was conducted to enable girls with disabilities to find their voice and fulfill their potential because they faced societal barriers and lost their voice. To stay alive, they indulged in substance abuse and other societal ills, became subservient, and eventually dropped out (*Living out Loud*, n.d.).

Yet another group of disabled students—delinquent youth—found themselves involved with the law. Although the NCLB provided for them, their education never received much attention. "For there is a general kind of benign neglect when it comes to this kind of population. It is almost viewed in some circles as a disposable population" (Gehring 2005, 3).

Continuous research studies have revealed the disproportionate number of minority students receiving inadequate education leaving them behind and unmarketable. As Viadero pointed out, teachers at times dismissed minority students from their classrooms because their actions gave the students a very negative message. Then these teachers, through colormuteness, ignored the students' cry for help. They allowed minority students to wander the halls undisturbed. Consequently, these students could not receive the intended instruction to move forward appropriately with their classmates. As a result, the students remained stigmatized with blame cast on their values, their parents, and on themselves. The confused and frustrated students felt that they were stereotyped, often ignored, and not given equal and appropriate treatment.

Similarly, Carroll (2008) reported that a growing number of schools were pushing young people, particularly minority, out of the classroom into the juvenile system. Although it cost $8,701 to educate a child in the United States and six times as much to incarcerate him/her, more African American males are in prison. In addition, African American students make up less than 1% of the student population and young people; nonetheless, they account for one-third of suspension, more likely to be referred to the justice system, and represent more than 13% of the prison population.

Roekel (2008) expressed chagrin over the public education system that allowed about 50% of young African American and Hispanic males not to get through school. He claimed that there was not equal access and opportunity for all students, showing that society could care less about some students. Yet other students attended beautiful schools, well equipped and modern in every way.

Samuels (2008) also informed that special-needs children are further left out by the under-eighteen-year-old law that decreased their protection.

Medication/Substance Abusers

A study done on human rights indicated that poor economic status gave rise to undernourishment, malnutrition, and diseases (Enable Human Rights and Disabled Persons 2003-04). In addition, Mendelson and Mello (1992, 1986) described students as being sick and lacking the ability to concentrate. In their study on psychoactive drugs, they established that alcohol depressed or slowed down the cells and organs of the body, rendering them less efficient. They found that many groups, including 90% of high school seniors, consumed alcohol for various reasons. Consequently, the students displayed characteristics such as low self-esteem, feelings of failure, and feelings of hopelessness, leading to inattentiveness and restlessness.

Accordingly, an unhealthy child could not grasp concepts or stay alert and awake to make any positive progress. Au contraire, "a healthy child is one who is well rested, alert, clear-headed, calm, and able to concentrate on the day's work, and just generally ready to attend to the work of the school. In contrast, an unhealthy student is one who is sick, high, speedy, and not ready to get at it." In other words, poor children lost the ability to make positive progress academically.

Haller (1999) emphasized that children in poor neighborhoods displaying hyperactive symptoms often received Ritalin to calm them down. The report outlined that this drug produced a feeling of euphoria in normal individuals and caused sleepiness, weight loss, irritability, nausea, dizziness, and headache while it helped control impulsiveness in some disadvantaged children and adults.

However, the research acknowledged that over 1.5 million children in the United States remained on this drug. Likewise, providers prescribed many other drugs besides Ritalin for children in order to control hyperactive behavior and reduce attention deficit disorder and/or minimal brain dysfunction (Morrison 2002; Wallace and McLoughlin 1988; Dodes 2002). These drugs included Ambien, Vicoden, Adderal, Xanax (stimulants), as well as easily attained substances such as alcohol, cough syrup, and flavored beer. Consequently, a drug culture emerged from the number of children using these drugs, which resulted in adverse effects such as dependency, overdosing, and, sometimes, death. Other researchers contended that parents, teachers, and service providers often could not determine the causes of the adverse effect and reaction. As a result, they misjudged, mislabeled, and misplaced these students. Doctors tried to help by prescribing more medication to curb these adverse reactions, which magnified the problem with side effects symptomatic to mental disorders (Morrison 2002; Daley 2002; Wilens 1999). The prescribed drug use led to usage of other substances such as painkillers, wine coolers, coffee, and nicotine in cigarettes (Morrison 2002; Wilens 1999; Mendelson and Mello 1992, 1986; Dodes 2002).

Moreover, depressive disorder, common in adolescents and previously thought of as merely excessive emotional turmoil tantamount to their normal development, caused illnesses in many children (Lonsdale 1996). Alternatively, when the children were diagnosed, parents refused the diagnosis and treatment (Morrison 2002). The doctors in denial then sided with parents and teachers and labeled the children lazy. Meanwhile, they hoped for a change as the children matured (Dodes 2002; Wilens 1999). Other students who had underlying diseases such as diabetes, hypothyroidism, hyperthyroidism, or some infectious diseases displayed signs of mental illness and became increasingly worse because their medical problems went unattended. They too became addicted to prescription drugs and displayed adverse reactions.

Similarly, food additives, dyes, or natural salicylates are major causes of hyperactivity and learning disabilities (Wallace and McLoughlin 1988, 1979, 1975). Researchers added that vitamins did not improve behavior or performance in learning-disabled students. Other reports confirmed that children who had allergic reaction to food often displayed symptoms compatible to mental disorder. They were often misdiagnosed and suffered continuously (Brostoff and Camblin 2000; Walsh 1995)

EXAMINATION FAUX PAS

Constraints

However, the state mandates and the NCLB Act warranted disadvantaged children be in the educational system until the age of twenty-one years old. Some researchers maintained that disadvantaged students had lower aspirations for further education (Wallace and McLoughlin 1988; *Living Out Loud*, n.d.; Schwarz 1995). Nevertheless, the Balanced Budget Act of 1997 and the Taxpayer Relief Act of 1977 have given many, including special-needs people, the perspective of pursuing higher education through HOPE Scholarship and Lifetime Learning Credits. This opened the doors of college to a new generation, with the largest investment in education in fifty years. The incentive promised a huge tax credit equal to 100 percent of the first $1,000 of tuition and fees and much more (ED Initiatives 1997).

The incentives generated an eagerness to push students to pursue higher education for the benefits. According to some reports, learning-disabled students who had problems taking notes, completing homework, and preparing for tests had to fulfill the HOPE dream, nonetheless. They continually made ineffective decisions and repetitive mistakes to guarantee the tax credit for the family (Davis 2004; Olsen 2004; Bartolomeo 2004; Robelen 2004).

Wolf (2005) affirmed that millions of children did not get quality education because public education was always about money. There were other reports stating that schools could not close the achievement gap between rich and poor students and reduce the dropout rate (Cowan 2005; Steedman 1997-2001).

However, the president's education agenda outlined goals ensuring every eight-year-old the ability to read, every twelve-year-old to log on to the Internet, every eighteen-year-old can go to college, and every adult to continue learning for a lifetime (ED Initiatives 2004).

The federal and state mandates, including the No Child Left Behind (NCLB) Act and the HOPE scholarship, also put tremendous pressure on special-needs children to pass standardized tests and exit exams. Hoff (2005) discovered that students from some states felt rushed to pass examinations in four major subjects in order to graduate. Confirming that study, Olsen (2005) indicated that some states enacted policies that required students to complete tougher academic programs with more courses in mathematics, science, and other core areas.

However, Ysseldyke, Nelson, Christenson, and Johnson (2005) in their empirical study found the following problems with testing and reporting. Some states did not include special education in their report of passes or failures. Special education students did not get to write for the tests. Subjective IEPs linked to statewide assessments and accountability system did not align with what the students learned. Only a checklist method determined the passing or failure of special education students; drill-and-practice teaching methods geared to improve performance on high stakes exam did not develop higher order thinking skills in students with disabilities.

The researchers also emphasized that conflict arose between complying with the laws and exposure for students with disabilities as it pertained to testing. In such instances, the students tackled the opportunity to learn the contents of the test but were unsure of the provisions for testing accommodations. Also, special needs children dropped out of high school because they feared the tests, claiming that the state tests were an 'insurmountable barrier' that took away their self-worth. Some parents even sued school districts that did not prepare the students adequately for the exams. They concluded that the high stakes exams caused a high percentage of high school dropouts among children with disabilities (Ysseldyke et al., 2005)

Another study confirmed the aforementioned where the researchers found that a disproportionate number of special needs students dropped out of school and experienced higher post school rates of incarceration, unemployment and underemployment (Sinclair, Christenson, Thurlow, 2005).

Furthermore, another report stated that only 11.84% of the 111,000 special education students enrolled in New York City schools (NYC) received a high school diploma in eight years 1996-97 to 2003-04.; 12% received IEP diplomas. The report concluded that although a tremendous amount of resources went into special education services, students with disabilities did not earn a Regents or local diploma (Samuels, 2005).

In order to comply with the NCLB mandates districts and schools have put much emphasis on standardized tests as part of the accountability component. However, Stock (2007) cautioned that struggling learners do not have a chance of competing successfully. Besides, Stock indicated the ramifications of such testing which allowed for only "One Right Answer," encouraging a standardized way of thinking. Such complacency, he claimed, disallowed creative thinking and challenge to other viable processes, giving rise to authoritarian rule.

The good thoughts of NCLB continued to be marred by additional problems as depicted by Miller (2008). In that report, Miller pointed out the issue with the "testing" where teachers indicated the disconnection with student. They aggrieved over the demands of NCLB that caused a breakdown in teacher-student relationship. The teachers stressed that the ramp up demands put on the testing activities allowed them little time to do justice to the subject matter with the student. They compared that situation to going to war unprepared. This was part of the NCLB qualification for schools that received Title I funding. Teachers complained that testing was taking the joy out of teaching because testing machines were unfamiliar and teachers were like little robots, jumping from student to student who experienced only four months per year without testing (Shaw 2008).

Push Up to Push Out

These researchers confirmed a previous study done by Schemo (2004) who reported an incident described by a sixteen-year-old special education student who claimed that the school wanted to get rid of her quickly. She complained that the school promoted her from one grade to the next whether or not she advanced academically. She added that her younger brothers learned important things like how to write in script, but she could not because the school never taught her to do so. She lamented, "That's all that matters to them at school, how to get rid of me." Her parents confirmed the student's accusation, stressing that the school continued to "push her up and move her on," but did not educate her. Schemo concluded that the quality of special education services available to students was "grossly inadequate." Gehring (2005) supported the finding when he proclaimed that schools, which were overwhelmed, had a "push out" and "keep out" program, which kept children with a label out of the schools.

Additionally, Samuels (2008) informed that students with the label "special education" and all its ramifications were often placed in self-contained classes and given instruction not as rigorous as their counterparts. Such disparities have been occurring to date.

9

UNPREPARED FOR INDEPENDENCE

BLATANT DISPARITIES

The evidence uncovered for this report illustrated that many factors including their neighborhood, self-esteem, and unqualified teacher oftentimes contributed to the neglect of the disadvantaged students. In the meantime, the unanswered questions continue to linger, are special-needs children prepared for independence and self-sufficiency or fulfilling the NCLB's mantra, closing the achievement gap?

The numerous aforementioned research addressing the lingering question showed that factors including inappropriate assessment and flawed placement, invalid placement and testing, incompetent and uncertified teachers, inconsistency with the laws (PL 94-142 IDEA 2005), and many other problems cited in this research impeded the progress of the special-needs students in the education process. Similarly, a grave situation depicted by Hale (2001) found that society subjugated the educational expectation for black boys and girls across all social and economic background.

Ysseldyke et al. (2005) in their study showed that a large number of special-needs children dropped out of school because of the pressure of the exit examinations that the state imposed on them. Similarly, Samuels (2005) reported that over an eight-year period, from school year 1996-97 to school year 2003-04, only 11.84% of special education students graduated in New York City. Others, the report claimed, dropped out, while 12% earned an IEP diploma. These reports supported earlier research warning that disabilities and their effects persisted into adulthood starting where special students lacked employability skills. Still other research denoted that those with unemployable skills often became crime victims or crime perpetrators who lived in subhuman conditions. As well, some could not earn their independence from adults.

However, the No Child Left Behind (NCLB) Act of 2001 stipulated that all children must be serviced equally. Nevertheless, Davis (2004) reported that the educational process did not serve special children adequately. Olsen (2005, 2004) claimed that states did what best serve their own purposes, which left out many disabled students in dire need of help. Eventually, according to the report, special education students who could not pass the mandated tests usually dropped out (Olsen 2005; Hoff 2005; Sinclair et al. 2005; Ysseldyke et al. 2005; Samuels 2005). Nevertheless, questions such as did the state-mandated tests affect special-needs children previously and how they are functioning as adults today prompted the present researcher to investigate further. What is the connection or how is special education associated mostly with African American students? Are African American—minority—special education students being served equally? Why are minorities—African Americans—given a broken vehicle to travel through the treacherous road to self-sufficiency and independence?

Past Graduates 1995-2003

Data/Survey

This investigator collected data about special education graduates from a school district with similar characteristics to District G in New York State. The researcher divided the participants, seniors in the year 1995-2003, into three groups. The study here was to compare and contrast the factors: number of students in each group of seniors, the number graduated, skills training received, and the relationship between the input and outcomes, the variables, especially the effect of mandated tests as depicted in figure 3. Group 1 represents the years 1995, 1996, and 1997 with 489 active students. Among them, 11% or 53 students were special education students. Of the 53 students, 85% graduated, and 15% moved, died, or dropped out. Among the graduates, 85% attended BOCES and learned a skill with 7% attending college. To date, all the graduates remain gainfully employed.

In the second group (1998, 1999, and 2000), there were 491 seniors. Of that number, 28 or 5% represented special-needs students, of which 71% graduated and 29% dropped out or died. Of the 71% who graduated,

32% attended BOCES and 10% attended college. All graduates are doing well in successful employment or higher education.

In the third group (2001, 2002, and 2003), there were 585 seniors. Of that number, 65 students or 11% represented students with disabilities. Fifty-three percent of the special-needs students graduated and 46% dropped out. Among the graduates, 21% attended BOCES and 1% attended college. All the graduates are employed today.

Figure 3

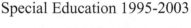

Special Education 1995-2003

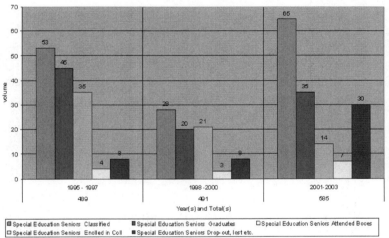

Discussion

On closer examination, this researcher discovered that Board of Cooperative Educational Services (BOCES) played a very important part in the students' plan to attend college and obtain a marketable employable skill. The researcher observed and interviewed the students and collected data from the school. The data also showed significant uses of the BOCES program in the earlier years than in the later years. In 1995-1997, more special education students graduated, fewer students dropped out, and more attended college than in the last three years.

Further scrutiny of the data indicated that the closer to the present year, the higher the dropout rate and the lower the graduate rate for special education students. Fifteen percent dropped out in years 1995-1997, a higher rate of 29% in 1998-2000, and the highest rate of 46% in 2001-2003. And 1% attended college in the last three years in contrast to 7% in 1995 and 10% in 2001-2003, with only 1% attending college in the last three years in contrast to 7% in 1995-1997 and 10% in 1998-2000. It was discouraging to find that out of sixty-five special education seniors in 2001-2003, a little less than half, 30% of the students, dropped out or were lost in the system. With mandates and laws in place to help the specials, the result ought to be the opposite or significantly more positive. Although not all the graduates attended, BOCES played a very important role in molding and preparing them for the future. As Hayden (2005) emphasized, "BOCES catches some students who would otherwise fall through the cracks of our educational system." He reported that a special student on the verge of dropping out followed his teacher's advice, attended BOCES, and became a successful teacher.

This data collected by the researcher about the past graduates posed a troubling picture, signifying that special education students lost interest in the educational process and finally dropped out during those years. The investigator then proceeded to look at other factors or sources that influenced the students so negatively. One of the factors pointed to the state and federal mandates that pertained to the requirements necessary for special education students and their future.

Executive Changes

The factor(s) that the researcher uncovered hinged on the new changes enacted by the state and federal governments. The changes dictated the implementation and enforcement of stipulated mandates known as education reform. The mandates also stated that most school reforms did not improve education. Instead, they bolstered the status of the district policy makers. In addition, many teachers and implementers testified they never tested innovations for efficacy before trial (Hu 2005).

Another change occurred in 1997 where the College Choice Tuition Savings Program encouraged families to save their children's college education by providing tax benefits or contributions to college savings account. The State Tuition Tax Credit and Deduction Program provided both a state tax credit and deduction for parents and students who wanted financing for college education (NYS 2004-05 Executive Budget: Education 2005).

In 1998, schools experienced tremendous pressure to initiate reform in secondary education outlined in the Comprehensive Whole School Reform. Included in the Whole School Program were the following:

- Increased students participation in class
- Higher proportion of students earning grades A or B

- Students' articulation of connection across the disciplines
- Climate of cooperation
- High rates of attendance
- Low discipline referral

Accordingly, education reform did not help poor black and disadvantaged children who did not receive strict content-based curriculum. Rather, the reforms addressed problems with the system that did not teach these particular students the same excellent way as white students were. Paring down of education became the norm for them. Consequently, they became the worst victims with the lowest scores on performance-based tests (Education Index, n.d.; Testing: Index of Diversity).

In the meantime, a report identified New York as the state that placed the most children in special education classes in the nation, thereby increasing state funds to 48 percent or more than twice the rate of inflation. The increased state funds automatically increased taxpayer support. To curb some of the financial spending, Governor Pataki amended the original STAR program to include a spending growth cap which protected taxpayers from excessive local school property tax increases. He also put a cap on school budget increases to lessen the burden of increasing property tax on homeowners. However, the executive Budget showed that school taxes continued to spiral upwards from 1998. And growth in local school taxes outpaced inflationary growth during 1998-2003. The governor outlined the following goals to help control New York State spending:

- Place disabled children in the regular classroom whenever appropriate
- Consolidate $2.2 billion in funding for public special education programs within Flex Aid
- Discontinue the allocation of aid based upon special education placements
- Limit statewide aid for private special education to a certain level
- Eliminate BOCES aid for routine administrative service
- Obtain approval from the Governor's office of Regulatory Reform before imposing new regulations by the Board of Regents (NYS 2004-05) Executive Budget: Education, 2005)

The reform concluded that by 2000 American high schools took advantage of vocational students because of the relentless focus on college preparation. Moreover, the President, in keeping with the new guidelines, declared that he wanted every student to get through high school and prepare for college.

Carroll (2008) reported that the alliance for Excellent Education indicated that more time and money be directed to the 1.2 million students who dropped out each year. That would allow more of them to earn high school diploma, saving the state $17 billion in health care costs over the graduates' lifetime. Also, pointedly, poor children who received high quality education had significantly fewer arrests than peers without an education.

Furthermore, Carroll explained, that state leaders would do a better job educating the disadvantaged if they worried "less about how many prison beds they have and concentrated more on improving the schools' and teaching.

10

COMPLEMENTARY STUDY

To complement the studies done by the numerous researchers mentioned, the originator of this study conducted another research to identify the variables and the impact of testing and preparation for independence.

In the spring of 2005, the researcher sent out 150 questionnaires to juniors and seniors to high schools in mid-Nassau County, Long Island, New York. Of the respondents, there were 74.9% juniors and 24.8% seniors. The target population was the 29.3% special education students. The participants consisted of Asian and Chinese, 3.1%; Hispanics, 31.25%; Haitian blacks, 18.75%; and African Americans, 46.8%—total blacks, 67.55%.

Figures 4 and 5 illustrated the outcome:-

DATA COLLECTION & ANALYSIS

Figure 4 shows the distribution of the respondents.

Survey Profile

		Actual	Responses Percentage	Percentage	Actual
Regular Education	Reg. Seniors	10	15.60%	15.60%	10
	Reg. Juniors	35	54.60%	54.60%	35
Special Education	Spec. Seniors	6	09.50%	09.50%	6
	Spec. Juniors	13	20.30%	20.30%	13
		64	100.00%	100.00%	64

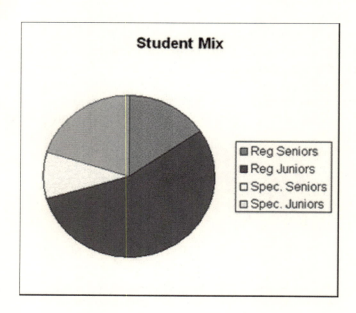

Figure 4

	Percentage (%)
African American	0.468
Hispanic	0.3125
Haitian	0.1875
Others (Indian, Asian, Italian)	0.032

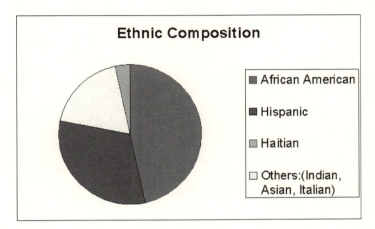

Figure 5

The data collected showed that the control group, as well as the target group, declared school, to some extent, did not prepare them for a job, to live on their own or self-sufficiency, as depicted in the tables 6, 7, 8, and 9.

Table 6

School role in preparation for independence

	Prepared Very Well	Prepared Somewhat	No Preparation
Regular Education (Control group)	0	90.60%	9.38%
Special Education (Target group)	0	52.90%	47.00%

Table 7

Regular education The extent to which schools help students to:	Very Well (%)	Average (%)	Little (%)	None (%)
Live on their own	5.9	30.4	33.1	29.5
Prepare for a job	21.8	46.8	18.7	12.7
Find a job	16.1	35.5	32.3	16.0
Special Education				
Live on their own	18.7	31.1	31.3	18.9
Prepare for a job	38.2	40.0	11.1	14.7
Find a job	10.0	40.0	23.3	26.26

The survey also showed that a large number, 81.2%, of the students with disabilities identified BOCES as the educational program that prepared them for independence. Whereas, 15.5% of the regular education students without disabilities expressed the same for BOCES.

Table 8

The students' goals after high school	Go to College	Get a Job	Learn a Trade	Cohabit
Regular Education (Control group)	65.9	30.4	8.7	5.0
Special Education (Target group)	11.0	36.5	52.3	0

Table 9

Students' thoughts on Regents exams

	Challenging (%)	Intimidating (%)	Serves No Purpose (%)	Avoid Exam (%)	Would Like to Drop Out (%)
Regular Education	33.50	40.00	20.00	7.50	6.50
Special Education	3.25	60.50	21.00	9.00	6.25

Discussion and Assumption

The survey indicated that schools did not adequately prepare students, especially the disabled, for employment or higher education. More special education students indicated that they wanted an opportunity to learn necessary life skills for survival. Moreover, they acknowledged BOCES as a comfortable learning environment that prepared them for independence.

Similarly, the 40% of special-needs students who wanted to attend college could have been regular education students who were misdiagnosed, incorrectly assessed, and misplaced, confirming previous studies of Hale (2002), Overton et al. (2004), Hosp and Reschly (2004), and Dodes et al. (2005).

Furthermore, the 52.3% and 36.5% of special education students who would have liked to learn a trade and get a job, respectively, indicated their preference in leaving school before the exit exams, describing the humiliating experiences of the exam as reported by similar previous studies by Olsen (2005, 2004) and Ysseldyke et al. (2005).

There was a significant drop from the junior special education student population to the senior class. It signified that the special education students dropped out before they entered the twelfth grade as depicted by figure 4.

Graduation 2008

Graduation in the United Stated in June 2008 as recorded in the Research Center confirmed the preceding research indicating the consequences of the inadequate education given to African American—minority—special education students. According to the 2008 graduation report, there were 4.18 million ninth graders, but only 2.95 million graduated in June 2008, depicting that high schools lost 6,829 students per day. Of the nearly 1.23 million students who failed to graduate, the analysis showed that most of them were African Americans and Latinos. As of 2005, there was a steady decrease in graduation where blacks led with the lowest percentage of graduates.

11

SUMMATION

DISCUSSION AND CONCLUSION

The purpose of this study was to provide information on the impact of juxtaposing special education with minority and to uncover the educational process imposed on these children in preparing them for employment, self-sufficiency, and productive citizenry.

Using data collected from eleven school districts, past students, case studies, observations, interviews, and a high school junior/senior survey in New York, this researcher's investigations demonstrate similar findings. For example, the eleven school districts showed that socioeconomics and demographics were significant factors influencing the percentage of Regents diplomas, college enrollment, dropout, and delegation of service to special students. They are consistent with the continuous findings from 1988 to today.

Likewise, this study depicts the more that 50% of special-needs students as minorities who attend schools in districts with low to median income, confirming previous reports including Davis et al. (2005), Overton et al. (2004), Hosp and Reschly (2004), Hale (2001), Cech (2007), Stock (2007), and Samuels (2008).

Furthermore, these minority students are also deprived of nutritious foods, which help enhance an alert mind, good thinking, and creative abilities. As Soledad O'Brien (2008) in her research "Black in America" demonstrated, black people in Harlem, New York, would have to travel miles away for fresh fruits, vegetables, and nutritious foods. Similar situation is seen in most minority neighborhoods where there are only processed foods, cheap foods, and packaged foods that have a very long shelf life. O'Brien stressed that people who wanted fresh foods and/or vegetables had to travel miles away to different communities for the same, very much unlike the children from a higher socioeconomic neighborhood.

As well, each classroom in these districts has more than thirty students where the teachers do not possess the required qualifications or the motivation to do so. This allows for inadequate and ineffective teaching, with students unfulfilling their IEPs or achieving their fullest potential, as well as increased burnout and attrition among their teachers.

On the other hand, the predominantly white student population in higher-income districts received continuous hands-on instruction from qualified teachers on a 20:1 student-to-teacher ratio basis. Accordingly, each of the teachers works in accompaniment with one or two qualified assistants. As a result, the students are motivated, became self-determined, and propelled to higher academia, consistent with the findings of Billingsley et al. (2004), Billingsley (2004), Karvonon et al. (2005), Naugaret et al. (2005), Samuels (2008), Tompkins (2008), and Viadero (2008).

The past students' record and junior/senior survey showed that students from the first group (1995-1997) who did not have to write for the Regents examination remained in school until completion. Ultimately, they obtained and kept a job. BOCES, in this case, gave many special students confidence, self-assurance, and self-determination and continued to enhance the quality of their lives. On the contrary, the state and federal mandates to pass a standardized test and the pressure to enroll in college increased the dropout rate among special students in the second and third groups, 1998-2000 and 2001-2003. This reiterates the findings of Olsen (2002, 2004), Gehring (2005), Hoff (2005), Samuels (2005), Griffin (1988), Jones (1981), Ferreyra (2001), Ysseldyke et al. (2005), and Miller (2008).

Although special education students are entitled to testing accommodations, the survey demonstrated that they preferred not to accept them because of the portrayal of incompetence. They also claimed that the test intimidated and served them no purpose. However, they preferred to learn a skill or trade where they can see practical results and continuous improvement and development of creativity through their eagerness to show their own craft. This, they explained, would make them feel important, competent, and accomplished, paralleling the studies done by Jenkins et al. (2003), Gates (2005), Karvonen et al. (2005), Torrey and Zdanozicz (n.d.), Reid et al. (2005), Stiggins (2007), Kolderie (2008), and Carroll (2008).

IMPLICATION

This investigation shows that most minority students/special education students do not receive appropriate and effective education, leaving them unemployable, dependent, frustrated, and worthless. The message is clear that many minority students are subjugated in the educational process by the following:

- The laws and ambiguous mandates, NCLB
- Funding
- Untrained personnel
- Pedantic attitudes toward them
- Inappropriate and inadequate instruction
- Dropout rate
- Poor nutrition/ill health
- Testing
- Politics

The tabula rasa that every child is given at birth means that every child can learn and should be given the opportunity to learn appropriately. That philosophy was proven and demonstrated in the Marva Collins School that was founded in 1975 and highlighted by Parylak. The school system was very successful—even turning a child labeled as "borderline mentally retarded" into a summa cum laude college graduate. Collins's model erased the unflattering labels given to students and developed a creed for teachers as well as students to follow strictly. The teachers' role included the following:

— Demonstrating enthusiasm in their respective field of study
— Encouraging every child's creative expression
— Stimulating each student's creativity
— Stressing the importance of each child's responsibility
— Caring about the student within and beyond the classroom

All the teachers had the responsibility to do whatever they could to draw out the students' motivation based on the following students' creed: "Likewise, if I want to fail, that too is my choice. Time and chance comes to us all. Whether I decide to take that time and chance is indeed my own choice . . . I can swiftly stand up and shout, *'This is my time and place. I will accept the challenge or I will let others make my decision for me.'*"

Unfortunately, minority students are repeatedly given the special education label, stripping them of their dignity and self-worth and subjugating them to substandard education.

The pattern emanating from the studies here is destructive to the minority student who is thrown into a cycle of inadequate education, absent parents, low self-esteem, no marketable skills, incarceration, teen pregnancy, illegitimate children, dependency, and ultimate liability to the government.

It stands to reason that it takes the minority student a long time to get out of the special education assessment and on a regular track. In the meantime, the other students would be duly educated in a regular environment with no stigma, stereotyping, or prejudged assessment. The mandates and law only help to further humiliate the minority student who is wedged among frustration, low self-esteem and unqualified teachers, and malnutrition.

Juxtaposing special education with minority students means that minority students are lacking the capability of learning without help. The help signifies subjugation and stereotyping. The subtle message implies that minority students are inferior and should be given equivalent education. They are then thrown into overcrowded classrooms with untrained teachers who are interested more in a paycheck and not in disseminating appropriate knowledge to the children. Teaching the minority special education students eventually becomes a custodial job, keeping the student in the classroom. Likewise, some of these students would do as they pleased, walk the halls, disrespect personnel, and cut classes without any consequences to them because they are "special." Special education students are not supposed to be punished or could remain in public school until twenty-one years old and would be forgiven.

Added to their dilemma, the minority student emerges from an environment where teen pregnancy is rampant. Positive role models are absent from their lives where most of the young adult males are incarcerated with no more than an eighth-grade education. Survival becomes the mantra of their lives, propelling them into criminal activities or minimum paying jobs that cannot cover their financial needs.

A product from such environment has to jump many, many hurdles to get to the finish line in time. Accordingly, the big beautiful bus—NCLB—has all the earmarks of working for all. However, it is loaded with invisible chains that would bound the minority child. Besides, the engine is broken, the tires are flat, and it can only go so far down the wrong path to a repetitive cycle to dependence, insufficiency, prison, and unfulfillment.

Recommendations:

It therefore incumbent upon the administrators, educators, parents, and teachers to make sure that all students—especially the special-needs, a.k.a. minority, students—receive an effective education to fulfill their potential, boost their self-esteem, and give them self-motivation and self-determination skills that would enable them continuous growth in dependence, self-reliance, and self-worth. This means that all personnel, including the community, should consider the following in developing and implementing programs for all children especially special-needs children who are mostly minority students:

- Needs should determine funding, not test scores.
- Secure trained personnel to assess and test and provide all services in a conducive environment mandatory.
- Place enough trained and certified teachers and service providers in low-income areas.
- Remove labels—treat all special-needs students as regular, normal people.
- Consider sensitivity to each child's uniqueness in testing and placement.
- Ensure that appropriate counseling be given at least three times per week or as needed.
- Provide relevant programs to each child's needs.
- Each child above age twelve must be actively involved in the designing of his/her IEP.
- Mandate more skills training versus college-bound programs for special students.
- Provide more teacher/student-friendly environment for teachers and students to work daily.
- Encourage more community and parental involvement in the district with special students.
- Motivate that special students should learn basic life and survival skills.
- IEP should be monitored, updated, and amended every six months to ensure that these students are receiving relevant and appropriate instruction.
- Ensure that special education teachers should be included in the planning of school policies that affect special education.
- Stipulate that equal treatment is given to all teachers including special education teachers in a building or district.

- Seek more support for special education teachers who have a very challenging job to perform.
- Guarantee that graduation from high school can be acquiring a craft, a trade, as well as diploma.

The public and parents should be proactive in the assessment and placement of their children instead of accepting a skewed education; they must make a concerted effort to break the cycle of misplacement and stereotyping of the minority children and be a positive example. In this way, minority students would be able to make pertinent decisions with their parents' help and input, build sound character, take responsibility for themselves, gain empowerment through employment, and become self-sufficient, independent, and productive.

Abbreviations

AAMI	African American Make Initiative
ADA	Americans with Disabilities Act
ADHD	attention deficit/hyperactivity disorder
AFT	American Federation of Teachers
BOCES	Board of Cooperative Educational Services
EPSDT	early periodic screening, diagnosis, and treatment
ESEA	Elementary and Secondary Education Act
ESL	English as a second language
FAPE	free appropriate public education
IDEA	Individuals with Disabilities Education Act
IEP	individual education plan
IWRP	individualized written rehabilitation plan
LD	learning disabled
LEA	local educational agencies
LRE	least restrictive environment
NAEP	National Assessment of Educational Progress
NCLB	No Child Left Behind
NYC	New York City
NYS	New York State
OBRA	Omnibus Budget Reconciliation Act
OT	occupational therapy
PIC	parent information center
PL	public law
PT	physical therapy
SED	State Education Department
SURR	schools under registration and review

Glossary

accommodations (*n.*): Adjustments.
addiction (*n.*): The habitual use of a substance.
administrator (*n.*): An executive or official of a business, institution, et al.
adolescent (*n.*): Youth; between childhood and maturity.
affluence (*n.*): Abundance of riches; wealth.
alcohol (*n.*): A brew or liquor containing an intoxicating active agent.
allergy (*n.*): Hypersensitivity to a specific substance (such as food dust, etc.) manifested in physiological disorders.
amendment (*n.*): Addition made in a law; constitution.
antisocial (*adj.*): Unfriendly.
attrition (*n.*): Loss of personnel in the normal course of events; retirement.
basics (*n.*): Necessary skills, needs, prerequisites, essentials.
black (*n.*): Dark-skinned descendant of African race.
budget (*n.*): Amount of money needed for a particular plan.
burnout (*v.*): Disintegrate; wear down.
challenging (*v.*): Confronting; threatening.
collaborate (*v.*): To work together.
colormuteness (*n.*) Turning a blind eye to the infractions committed by black students.
compliance (*n.*): Readiness to accept meekly and without question.
confusion (*n.*): Puzzlement; perplexity; befuddlement.
consistency (*n.*): Uniformity; harmony.
contemporary (*adj.*): Of present or recent time; modern.
cooperate (*v.*): To work together for a common purpose.
counselor (*n.*): One who advises students.
curriculum (*n.*): Courses collectively offered in a school.
deinstitutionalize (*v.*): To remove from a treatment facility.

delinquent *(adj.)*: Failing or neglecting to do what the law requires faulty; derelict.
demographics *(n.)*: Characteristics of a population in race; habits.
depressed *(adj.)*: Gloomy; dejected.
disadvantaged *(adj.)*: Deprived of a decent standard of living and/or education.
discriminate *(v.)*: Divide; distinguish.
disproportionate *(adj.)*: Not symmetrical one faction doing more or less than the others.
diversity *(n.)*: Difference; different races existing together.
effectiveness *(adj.)*: Adequate; sufficient; competent.
empowerment *(n.)*: Authority; entitlement.
endanger *(v.)*: Jeopardize; expose; risk.
equality *(n.)*: Similarity; sameness; uniformity.
ethnicity *(n.)*: Determination of a group of human beings whose members identify with each other.
exceptional *(adj.)*: Above average; not ordinary.
expectation *(n.)*: Looking forward.
failure *(n.)*: Falling short; not succeeding.
food additives *(n.)*: Substance added to food to produce a desired effect.
frustrated *(adj.)*: Disappointed expectations and thwarted ambitions.
funding *(v.)*: Providing a fund for the payment of the interest or principal of a debt.
grant *(n.)*: Something granted as a privilege or right; a sum of money.
hallway *(n.)*: Passageway; corridor.
identification *(n.)*: The act of designating or acknowledging something or someone.
impulsive *(adj.)*: Thoughtless; hasty; sudden; emotional.
incarcerate *(v)*: Jail; imprison; confine.
inclusion *(n.)*: A program where special education and regular students receive academic services in a regular classroom.
incompetent *(adj.)*: Unskilled; incapable; inept.
independent *(adj.)*: Inner directed; individualistic; free.
individualize *(v.)*: To give special attention to the unique needs to each child.
institutionalize *(v.)*: To place in an institution for treatment.
intervention *(n.)*: Interference in the affairs of others.
intimidate *(v.)*: Frighten; scare; bully.
juniors *(n.)*: The year before graduating from high school.
label *(n.)*: Tags; stereotype. *(v.)* To classify; to identify; to brand.
legal *(adj.)*: Based on law; permitted by law; legitimate.

lingering (*adj.*): Bothersome; unclear; not easily perceptive.
linguistic (*n.*): The scientific study of language.
mainstreaming (*n.*): Placement of disabled people into regular school class, work, etc.
malnourished (*adj.*): Affected by improper nutrition or an insufficient diet.
manipulation (*n.*): A skillful handling.
misdiagnose (*v.*): To an incorrect diagnosis of a disease condition, etc.
nausea (*n.*): Queasiness; upset stomach.
nutrition (*n.*): Wholesome healthful food.
organs (*n.*): A distinct part of an organism that performs one or more specialized functions.
overwhelmed (*adj.*): Overcome; submerged; inundated.
performance (*n.*): Fulfillment of duties or obligations.
politics (*n.*): Artful actions; shrewd displays; diplomatic ploys.
potential (*n.*): Realizable future.
poverty (*n.*): Deficiency in necessary needs; destitution; penniless.
pressure (*n.*): Coercion; duress; harassment; force.
professional (*adj.*): Worthy of high standard.
providers (*n.*): Nurturers that support those in need.
public school (*n.*): Free educational facility maintained by people's taxes and supervised by local authorities.
quality (*n.*): The degree of excellence; of what kind.
quality (*n.*): An undetermined bulk; an amount; weight or number.
race (*n.*): Different varieties of human beings distinguished by physical traits.
reduced lunch (*n.*): Meal given to student in low-income districts.
Regents (*n.*): State system; governing board of institution.
rehabilitation (*n.*): Restoration of rank.
rejection (*n.*): Castoff; thrown away; abandonment.
resilient (*adj.*): Recovering strength; bouncing back.
resource (*n.*): Something that lies ready for use or that can be drawn upon for aid or take care of a need.
retention (*n.*): Ability to remember; possession holding; custody.
risk factors (*n.*): A risk factor is a variable that associated with the prolonging of a disease or infection.
Ritalin (*n.*): Stimulant used to lessen depression in children; hyperactivity.
secondary (*n.*): Of minor or lesser importance; subordinate.
segregation (*n.*): Practice of compelling racial groups to live apart.
self-contained (*adj.*): Remaining in the same classroom or teacher for the duration of the school year.

self-determination (*n.*): Decision according to one's own mind or will without outside influence.
self-esteem (*n.*): Belief in oneself; pride in oneself.
self-motivation (*n.*): Initiative to undertake or continue a task or activity without another's prodding or supervision.
socioeconomics (*n.*): The study of the interrelation between economics and social behavior.
special education (*n.*): Education that is modified or particularized for those having singular needs or disabilities as handicapped or maladjusted people, slow learners, or gifted children.
standardized test (*n.*): One that is administered under regulations or rules or controlled conditions that specify where, when, how, and for how long children may respond to the questions or "prompts."
state mandate (*n.*): Mandatory specification outlined by the state(s).
stereotype (*n.*): Fixed conception of a person, group; idea held by a number of people; any of a large class of organic compounds having as a basis 17 carbon atoms.
steroids (*n.*): Arranged in four rings fused together.
subjugate (*v.*): To bring under control or submission.
subservient (*adj.*): Performing useful help in inferior or subordinate capacity.
suburbs (*n.*): Residential districts near the outside outskirts of the city; separately incorporated city or town.
sufficiency (*n.*): Adequate amount or quantity.
survival (*n.*): The act or fact of surviving, esp. under adverse or unusual circumstances.
suspension (*n.*): Barring from; temporary abrogation or withholding as of a law, privilege, decision, belief.
technology (*n.*): The science or study of the practical or industrial arts, applied sciences, etc.
therapy (*n.*): The treatment or disease or any physical or mental disorder by medical or physical means.
uncertified (*adj.*): Without the license or certificate required to perform the duty effectively.
underachievement (*v.*): To fail to do as well in school studies as might be expected from scores made on intelligence tests.
undermined (*v.*): Wear away and weaken the supports.
unhealthy (*adj.*): Harmful to health; harmful to morals or character.
urban (*adj.*): Characteristic of the city as distinguished from the country.
vegetable (*n.*): Plant that can be eaten raw with much nutritious value to health.

vocational (*adj.*): Intended to prepare one for an occupation sometimes specific in a trade.

weakness (*n.*): Shortcoming; feebleness; debility; vulnerability.

welfare recipient (*n.*): Someone who receives government aid because of poverty, unemployment, etc.

yearly (*adj.*): Annually; happening once in a year.

youth (*n.*): Puberty; being vigorous and lively; adolescence; immature; period of life coming between childhood and maturity.

zip code (*n.*): A code of letters and digits added to a postal address to aid in the sorting of mail.

References

Ainscow, M. Tweddle, D. A. 1979. Preventing classroom failure: An objective approach. New York: John Wiley and Sons Ltd.

Appalachia Educational Laboratory. (c) 1996-2005. Preventing antisocial behavior in disabled and at risk students. Retrieved May 11, 2005, from www.ldonline.org/ld_indepth/add_adhd/ael_behavior.html.

Are equality rights Arguments Essential Within the Debate of Bioethics Issues? n.d. Retrieved May 11, 2005, from http://www.thalidomide.ca/gwolbring/is.htm.

Background and history. n.d. Retrieved February 7, 2005, from http://www.ncld.org/advocacy/fedlaws.cfm

Bartolomeo, C. 2004. The funding divide. American Teacher, November 89 (3) p. 6.

Behrmann, M., and Jerome, M. 2002. *Assistive Technology for Students with Mild Disabilities*. ERIC Digest.

Billingsley, B., E. Carlson, and S. Klein. 2004. The working conditions and induction support of early career special educators. Spring 70 (3): 347.

Billingsley, B. S. 2004. Promoting teacher quality and retention in special education. *Journal of Learning Disabilities*. September/October 37 (3): 370-376.

Blankenship, C., and M. S. Lily. 1981. Mainstreaming students with learning and behavior problems. Saunders College Publishing: Holt Rinehart and Winston.

Brooks, P. H. 1989 (updated November 5, 2001). Special education inclusion. Retrieved May 9, 2005, from http://www.weac.org/resource/Jun96/specialed.htm.

Brostoff, J. and L. Gamlin. 1998, 1992, 2000. Food allergies and food intolerance: The complete guide to their identification and treatment.

Bussing, R., B. Zima, and A. Perwien. 2000. Self-esteem in special education children with ADHD: Relationship to disorder characteristics and medication use. *Journal of the American Academy of Child and Adolescent Psychiatry*, 39 (10): 1260.

Carroll, T. 2008, Education beats incarceration. Education Week, 27 (29): 1.

Cech, S. J. 2007, October 31. Ed. dept. holds firm on racial—data rules. Education Week, 27 (10): 19.

—. 2007, October 31. Georgia touts push to send more black makes to college. Education Week, 26 (15): 9.

Cowan, A. 2005. Amid affluence a struggle over special education. *New York Times*, Vol. CL1V. No. 53, 194: 37

Crattu, B. J., and R. L. Goldman. 1996. Learning disabilities: Contemporary viewpoints. Amsterdam: Harwood Academic Publishers.

Daley, D. 1991. Kicking addictive habits once and for all. San Francisco: Jossey—Bass.

Davis, Fox, W. Grage, and S. Gehshan. 2005. Deinstitutionalization of persons with developmental disabilities: A technical assistance report for legislators. Retrieved May 5, 2005, from http://www.ncsl.org/programs/health/forum/pub6683.htm.

Davis, M. R. 2004. Special ed teachers behind on compliance with law, GAO says. Deinstitutionalization. Retrieved May 5, 2005, from http://www.sciam.com/article.cfm?colID=19andarticleID=0002177C-B688-1DC9-AF71809EC588EEDF.

Dodes, L. 2002. The heart of addiction. New York: Harper Collins Publishers.

Dyson, L. 1992. Partnership: An innovative curriculum for disaffected and disadvantaged pupils. Great Britain: David Fulton Publishers.

ED Initiatives. 1997. Retrieved April 12, 2005, from http://www.ed.gov/pubs/ED Initiatives.

EPE Research Center. 2008, June 5. Graduation in the U.S. Education Week, 27 (40) 34. Education Week, July 28; 23 (43), 7.

Elementary and Secondary Education Act. n.d. Retrieved February 20, 2005, from http://www.ed.gov/policy/elsec/leg/esea02/beginning.html.

Enable Human Rights and Disabled Persons. 2003-04. Retrieved May 11, 2005, from United Nations Web site: http:www.un.org/esa/socdev/enable/dispaperdes0.htm.

Ferreyra, N. 2001. March-April, Issue No. 7. Disability world living out loud: Building resiliency in adolescent girls with disabilities. Retrieved May 11, 2005, from http://www.disabilityworld.org/03-04_01/women/10/.shtml.

Fuller, Torrey, and Zdanowicz, M. T. July 9, 1999. Deinstitutionalization hasn't worked. *Washington Post*. Retrieved May 4, 2005, from http://www.coc.cc.ca.us/departments/english/davis_d/deinstitutionalization.html.

Gates, B. 2005. High schools must change radically. Newsday, March 2. p. A35.

Gehring, J. 2005, July 27. NCLB's mandates on delinquent youths get attention. Education Week, 24 (43): 3.

Goodman, L., and Mann, L. 1976. Learning disabilities in the secondary school: Issues and practices. New York: Grune and Stratton.

Greene, L. J. 1986. Kids who underachieve. New York: Simon & Schuster.

Greenehouse, L. 2005. Does the disability act stop at the shoreline? *New York Times*. Vol. CL1V No. 53, 159.6.Tr.

Griffin, R. S. 1988. Underachievers in secondary school: Education off the mark.

Hale, J. E. 2001. Learning while black: Creating educational excellence for African-American children. Johns Hopkins University Press.

Haller, M. C. 1999. Learning disabilities 101: A primer for parents. Florida: Rainbow Books.

Harte, A. 2004. An uphill battle. Disabilities Awareness, 7, p. 2.

Hayden, T. 2005. Because of BOCES, I went from truant . . . to teacher. New York Teacher, March 31, p. 9.

Hilderbrand, J. 2005. Schools sweating over report cards.

Hirsch, E. D., Jr. 1996. The schools we need and why we don't have them. New York Doubleday.

Hoff, D. 2005, June 9. Schools feel pressure of efforts to increase fiscal accountability. Education Week, 24 (39): 1.

—. 2007, October 17. Bush, others want law to go beyond basics. Education Week, 27 (8): 18.

—. 2007, December 5. Usually contentions Title 1 formula is no NCLB barrier. Education Week, 27 (14): 18.

—. 2008, March 26. State gets flexibility on targets. Education Week, 27 (29): 1.

Hoff, D. J., and M. Walsh. 2008. Sparring on NCLB legal ruling continues. Education Week, 27 (21): 19.

Hosp, J. L., and D. J. Reschly. 2004. Disproportionate representation of minority students in special education: Academic, demographic and economic predictors: Exceptional Children, Winter, 70 (2), 185-197. http://www.crf-usa.org/brown50th/disabeled_students.htm.

Hu, A. n.d. Retrieved April 12, 2005, from http://www.arthurhu.com/index/edindex2.htm.

—. n.d. Testing index of diversity. Retrieved May 16, 2005, from http://www.arthurhu.com/index/test.htm.

Incarceration without rehabilitation in significant court cases. n.d. Retrieved May 11, 2005, from http://www.mvcc.edu/mvccinfo/edtech/dimeo/hs213/2court/sldo14.htm

Including the disabled student. n.d. Retrieved May 11, 2005, from Constitutional Rights Foundation Web site.

Jacobsen, L. 2005, June 22. Survey finds teachers' biggest challenge is parents. Education Week, 24 (41): 5.

Jenkins, J., L. Antil, S. Wayne, and P. Vadasy, eds. Spring 2003. How cooperative learning works for special education and remedial students. Exceptional Children, Vol. 69 i 3 (14).

Johnson, K. R. 1970. Culturally disadvantaged: A rational approach. Research Associates.

Jones, M. 1981. Exploring careers in special education. New York: Richards Rosen Press.

Karvonen, M., D. Test, W. Wood, D. Browder, and B. Algozzine, eds. Fall 2004. Putting self-determination into practice. Exceptional Children (Vols. 71 1) 23-41.

Kaye, S. 2005. Importance of funding is not rocket science. New York Teacher, April 14, 7.

Kolderie, T. 2008, March 12. Beyond system reform: The need for greater innovation in school and schooling. Education Week, 27 (27): 36.

Law and exceptional students. n.d. Retrieved May 7, 2005, from http://www.unc.edu/~ahowell/exceplaw.html.

Law and persons with disabilities. n.d. Retrieved May 11, 2005, from http://www.mvcc.edu/mvccinfo/edtech/dimeo/hs213/2court/sld001.htm.

Lehrer. n.d. The effect of mainstreaming on stereotypic conceptions of the handicapped.

Levine, M., and G. D. Askins. 2004. Is the lazy student a myth? American Teacher, October, p. 4.

Lonsdale, J. 1996. The Hatherleigh guide to child and adolescent therapy. New York: Hatherleigh Press.

Lynch, R. G. 2004. Preschool pays: High quality early education would save billions. American Educator, Winter, p. 26.

Mainstreaming in classrooms. n.d. Kids Health for Kids. Retrieved May 9, 2005, from http://www.kidshealth.org/kid/feeling/school/mainstreaming.html.

Manzo, K. K., and S. Cavanagh. 2007, November 28. Students in urban districts inching forward. Education Week, 27 (13): 8.

Martin, J. 2003. Grants and special projects (GASP). Retrieved May 11, 2005, from http://www.ou.edu/education/ersb/index.html.

McCubbin, H. I., M. A. McCubbin, A. I. Thompson, S. Y. Han, and C. T. Allen. 1997. Families under stress: What makes them resilient. Retrieved May 11, 2005, from http://www.cyfernet.org/research/resilient.html.

McGarth, D. 2007, November 28. Respecting teachers. Education Week, 27 (13): 27.

McNamara, B. E. 1998. Learning disabilities: Appropriate practices for diverse population. Albany, New York: State University of NY Press.

McNeil, M. 2008, September 24. States cite capacity gap in aid for schools on NCLB. Education Week, 28 (5): 10.

McPherson, S. April 29, 2005. Freedom daily equal rights for the disabled, indeed. Retrieved May 11, 2005, from http://www.fff.org/freedom/fd0501d.asp.

Medina, J. 2005. Judge dismisses suit seeking school aid. *New York Times*, February 20, Vol. CL1V, (53, 131) L 15.

Mendelson, J., and N. Mello. 1996, 1992. The encyclopedia of psychoactive drugs alcohol and alcoholism. Harvard University Medical School: Chelsea House Publishers.

Merrow, J. 2007, December 5. Learning without loopholes. Education Week, 27 (14): 36.

Morrison, J. 2002. Straight talk about your mental health: Everything you need to know to make smart decisions. Lawrence Erlbaum Associates.

Miller, R. 2008, October. Testing the joy out of education. American Teaher, 93 (2): 11.

Muscott, H., and S. O'Brien. 1999. *Teaching character education to students with behavioral and learning disabilities through mentoring relationships*. Retrieved September 16, 2005, from http://www.servicelearning.org/lib_svcs/lib_cat/index.php?library_id=4772&printable=1.

Neira, M. 2004. Union seeks streamlining for special ed formula. NYS United Teachers, October 21, p. 3.

Nettleton, S. 2004. Making a difference. Disabilities Awareness, Vol. 7, p. 3.

Neufeldt, V., and D. Guralnik. 1997, 1996. Webster's New World College Dictionary (3rd Ed). New York: Simon & Schuster McMillan Company. Newsday, March 9, p. A6.

Nougaret, A., T. Scruggs, and M. Mastropieri, eds. Spring 2005. Does teacher education produce better special education teachers? Exceptional Children Vols. 71 (3) 217-229.

NYC and NY State Schools Districts. n.d. Retrieved May 11, 2005, from http://www.emsc.nysef.gov/reperd2003/links/c28-dist.html.

NYS 2004-05 executive budget: Education. n.d. Retrieved April 12, 2005, from http://www.budget.state.ny.us/archive/fy0405archive/fy0405littlebook/education.html.

NYSED report card. Retrieved on May 11, 2005 from www.Emsc.nysed.gov/repcrd2003/link.

O'Brien, S. 2008, July 24. Black in America. Documentary. CNN News.

Olsen, L. 2004. No Child Left Behind Act changes weighed. Education Week, September 22; 24 (4): 31-34.

—. 2005, July 13. Requests win more leeway under NCLB. Education Week, 24 (42): 1.

—. 2005, June 22. States raise bar for high school diploma. Education Week, 24 (41): 1.

Overton, T., C. Fielding, and M. Simonson. 2004. Decision making in determining eligibility of culturally and linguistically diverse learners: Reasons given by assessment personnel. *Journal of Learning Disabilities*, July/August; 37, (4): 319-329.

Packard, V. 1983. Our endangered children growing up in a changing world. Boston; Toronto: Little Brown and Company.

Paglin, C. 2004. Practicing prevention: How one school district helps students avoid reading failure. American Educator, Fall, p. 20.

Parylak, L. 2002. Philosophical orientation and philosophers on education. Retrieved February 26, 2009, from http://www.easternnct.edu/depts/edu/textbooks/philcollins.html.

Paul, J., A. Turnbull, and W. Cruickshank. 1977. Mainstreaming: A practical guide. New York: Syracuse University Press.

PL 94-142 IDEA-Individuals with Disabilities Act. Retrieved February 7, 2005, from http://www.people.uncw.edu/fischettij/ashley.htm.

Public laws regarding special education. n.d. Retrieved May 7, 2005, from http://www.home.inreach.com/torsi/publiclaws.html.

Rabb, T. K. 2007, November 28. Assessments and standards: The case of history. Education Week, 27 (13): 36.

Reid, R., A. Trout, and M. Schartz, eds. Summer 2005. Self-regulation interventions for children with attention deficit/hyperactivity disorder. Exceptional Children Vols. 71 (4): 362-377.

Risk and resiliency factors. n.d. Retrieved May 11, 2005, from http://www.tyc.state.tx.us/prevention/riskfact.html.

Robelen, E. 2004, September 22. Kennedy bill would give states, district leeway. Education Week, 24, 4: 21, 31.

Robelen, E. W., and A. Klein. 2007, December 5. Effort for education as campaign issue fight for traction. Education Week, 27 (14): 1.

Rockel, V. 2008, September. NEA RA sets sight on leaders. *NEA Today*.

Rose, M. 2005, March. School finance in the "quality courts" spotlight. American Teacher, March 89 (6): 9.

Sager, R. 2004, September. In the N.Y. schoolhouse door: Blatant public school racism—right here in New York. *New York Post*, 28; p. 31.

Sametz, L., and C. S. McLaughlin. 1985. Educators, children and the law. Springfield, Illinois: Charles C. Thomas Publishers.

Samuels, C. A. 2007, December 12. Minorities in special education studied by U.S. panel: Civil Rights Commission to recommend steps on disproportionality issue. Education Week, 27 (15): 18.

—. 2008. September 24. Changes to Disabilities Act seen as offering students protection. Education Week, 28 (5).

—. 2008, January 30. Some states shift IEP burden of proof to school districts. Education Week, 27 (21): 1, 13.

—. 2008, March 19. Study finds Section 504 rules source of confusion for schools. Education Week, 27 (28): 1.

Samuels, C. 2005, June 15. Report raps NYC special education graduation rate. Education Week, 24 (40): 6.

Saunders, S. 2005, March. Seeking a better plan for special ed kids. New York Teacher, 17, p. 14.

Schemo, D. J. 2004. Parts of special-ed bill would shift more power to states and school districts. *New York Times*, November 22; Vol. CLIV (53,041), A22.

Schwarz, R., and M. Burt. January 1995. Digest ESL instruction for learning disabled adults. Retrieved May 11, 2005, from http://www.cal.org/caela/digests/Schwarz.htm.

Science Daily: Willowbrook State School. n.d. Retrieved February 9, 2005, from http://www.sciencedaily.com/encyclopedia/willowbrook_State_School.

Seltzer, E. 1997-2000. Information avenue archives: The mainstream child looking beyond academics. Retrieved May 9, 2005, from http://www.specialchild/com/archives/la-032.html.

Shaw, B. 2008, March 12. Our nation still at risk. Education Week, 27 (27): 26.

Sinclair, M., S. Christenson, and M. Thurlow. Summer 2005. Promoting completion of urban secondary youth with emotional or behavioral disabilities. Exceptional Children Vols. 71 (1): 23-41.

Skawinski, T. 2004. A teacher's perspective on education. Disabilities Awareness. Vol. 7. p. 4.

Standard & Poor's. Spring 2005. Outperforming School Districts of New York, 2002-2003. Retrieved from www.schoolmatters.com database.

Staten Island Advance. Thursday, May 8, 2003. Willowbrook school panel: Keep fighting for the disabled. Retrieved May 5, 2005, from http://www.csinews.net/IntheNews/050803csisip.htm.

Steedman, W. 1997-2001. Legal Files Archives—Inclusion. Retrieved May, 9, 2005, from http://www.specialchild.com/archives/lf-012.html.

Steely, S. n.d. Using folktales to examine justice and fair play: Exploring self-determination skill with students with special needs. Retrieved May 11, 2005, from http://www.unm.edu/~abqteach/justice/02-04-10.htm.

Stiggings, R. 2007, October 17. Five assessment myths and their consequences. Education Week, 27 (8): 28.

Stock, B. M. 2007, October 17. Not who but what is left behind. Education Week, 27 (2): 28.

Strachan, J. 2004, October. Math scores rise: Will funding follow suit? Official Publication of New York State United Teachers, 21; p. 3.

Strain, P. S., and M. M. Kerr. 1981. Mainstreaming of children in schools: Research and programmatic issues. London: Academic Press.

Supovitz, J. 2007, November 28. Why we need district-based reform. Education Week, 27 (13): 27.

Swanson, H. L., M. Hoskyn, and C. Lee. 1999. Interventions for students with learning disabilities. New York: Guilford Press.

Testing: Index of diversity. n.d. Retrieved May 16, 2005, from http://www.arthurhu.com/index/test.htm.

Tilstone, C. 1988. Teaching pupils with severe learning difficulties: Practical approach. London: David Fulton Publishers.

Tompkins, R. B. 2008, January 16. Rural schools: Growing diverse and complicated. Education Week, 27 (19): 24.

Tools for student success. n.d. Retrieved May 30, 2005, from http://www.ed.gov/parents/academic/help/tools-for-success/tools-for-success.

Torrey, E., and M. Zdanowicz. Deinstitutionalization hasn't worked. Retrieved May 4, 2005, from http://www.coc.cc.ca.us/department.english/davis_d/deinstitutionalization.htm.

Truscott, S. D., J. Meyers, B. Meyers, L. M. Gelzheiser, and C. B. Grout. 2004, Fall. Do shared decision making teams discuss special education in education reform meetings? *Journal of Disability Policy Studies*, 15(2) 112.

Van Osdal, B. M., and P. Perryman. 1974. Special education: A new look. New York: MSS Information Corporation.

Viadero, D. 2008, January 30. Teachers advised to "get real" on race. Education Week, 27 (21): 1.

Wallace, G., and J. A. McLoughlin, 1988. Learning disabilities concept and characteristics (3rd Ed.). Columbus; Toronto; London: Merrill Publishing Company.

Walsh, M. 2007, October 17. Court is split on IDEA private-placement case. Education Week, 27 (8): 18, 22.

Walsh, W. 1995. The food allergy book: The foods that cause you pain and discomfort and how to keep them out of your diet.

Wieselthier V., and M. Allen. 1999, August 5. Forced treatment doesn't work. Retrieved May 4, 2005, from *Washington Post*: http://www.coc.cc.ca.us/departments/english/davis_d/forcedtreatment-html.

Wilens, T. 1999. Straight talk about psychiatric medications for kids. New York: Guildford Press.

Willowbrook Consent Decree. n.d. Retrieved May 5, 2005, from http://www.mvcc.edu/mvccinfo/edtech/dimeo/hs 213/2 court/sld 020.htm.

Wolk, A. 2005, April 17. What's a good education. Newsday, p. 48.

Woolfolk, A. 1998. Educational psychology (7th ed.): Law and exceptional students. Needham Heights, MA: Allyn Bacon.

World T.E.A.M. Sports. 2002. Retrieved September 16, 2005, from http://newfirstsearch.oclc.org/bZF/SPage?page name=record:pagetype = print:entityprinti"'.

Ysseldyke, J., J. Nelson, S. Christenson, and D. Johnson, eds. 2004, Fall. What we know and need to know the consequences of high-states testing for students with disabilities. Exceptional Children 71 (1): 75-94.

Zernike, K. 2005. The difference between steroids and Ritalin is. *New York Times*. Vol. CL1V (53): 159.

Index

A

ADA (Americans with Disabilities Act), 26, 35
ADHD (attention deficit/hyperactivity disorder), 70, 97–98, 129–30, 134
AFT (American Federation of Teachers), 26, 36, 39
alcohol, 98
Amateur Sports Act, 25
American Federation of Teachers, 26, 36, 39
Asperger's syndrome, 36
attention deficit/hyperactivity disorder, 70, 97–98, 130, 134

B

Balanced Budget Act of 1997, 99
Bioethics, 15, 129
BOCES (Board of Cooperative Educational Services).
    See Board of Cooperative Educational Services
Bureau of the Handicapped, 17

C

Carl D. Perkins Vocational and Applied Technology Education Act, 26
Child Care and Development Block Grant Act, 27
civil rights advocates, 13, 21
Civil Rights Commission, 33, 135
College Choice Tuition Savings Program, 106
colormuteness, 34, 53, 97
consent decree, 19–20

D

deinstitutionalization, 15, 21, 30
Developmental Disabilities Assistance and Bill of Rights Act, 20, 27

E

Early Intervention Amendments, 26
Education for All Handicapped Children Act, 20, 28
Education of the Handicapped Act

Amendments of 1983, 25, 28
Education of the Handicapped Act
 Amendments of 1986, 25
Education of the Handicapped
 Act Amendments of 1990.
 See IDEA (Individuals with
 Disabilities Education Act)
education reforms, 60, 106–7
Elementary and Secondary
 Education Act, 17, 29
ESEA (Elementary and Secondary
 Education Act). *See* Elementary
 and Secondary Education Act

F

FAPE (free appropriate public
 education), 17, 26–28
food additives, 99, 124
Fourteenth Amendment, 9, 14, 18–19
free appropriate public education, 17,
 26–28

H

Handicapped Children's Protection
 Act, 25, 60
high objective uniform state standard
 of evaluation, 39
HOPE Scholarship and Lifetime
 Learning Credits, 100
HOUSSE (high objective uniform
 state standard of evaluation), 39

I

IDEA (Individuals with Disabilities
 Education Act), 14, 22, 24–25,
 27, 37–39, 58, 66, 103
IEP (individual education plan),
 26–28

IFSP (individualized family service
 plan), 26, 28
individualized education plan. *See*
 individual education plan
individualized written rehabilitation
 plan, 27
Individuals with Disabilities
 Education Act, 14, 22, 24–28,
 37–39, 58, 66, 88, 103
International Bill of Human Rights,
 17
IWRP (individualized written
 rehabilitation plan), 27

L

LEA (local educational agencies), 18
local educational agencies, 18
LRE (least restrictive environment),
 9–10, 18–20, 24, 26, 28, 35, 37, 66

M

Marva Collins School, 117
Medicare Catastrophic Coverage Act,
 26, 28
minorities, 3, 9–11, 13, 15–16, 22,
 31, 33–35, 50–51, 53, 62, 82,
 91–93, 95–97, 104, 114–15,
 117–20. *See also* special
 education: students

N

NCLB (No Child Left Behind) Act,
 10, 13–14, 16, 29, 39, 56–57,
 87, 89, 93, 95, 97, 100–101,
 104, 117–18, 133–34
New York State, 19, 54–55, 104
No Child Left Behind Act, 16, 29,
 39, 87, 89, 95, 134

O

OBRA (Omnibus Budget Reconciliation Act), 27
Omnibus Budget Reconciliation Act, 27

P

Paige, Rod, 24

R

Rehabilitation Act Amendment of 1992, 27
Rehabilitation Act of 1973, 58
resiliency, 22–23, 25, 134
Ritalin, 98, 137
Rivera, Geraldo, 19
Robin Hood approach, 56

S

schools under registration and review, 92–93, 96
Section 504, 26, 58
self-esteem, 10, 64, 68–70, 92
self-motivation, 9, 119
socioeconomics, 53, 91, 115
special education
  budget, 58–59
  classes, 13, 31, 34
  court cases
    Burham v. Georgia, 18
    Halderman v. Pennhurst, 18
    Jackson v. Indiana, 18
    Mills v. Board of Education of the District of Columbia, 19
    O'Connor v. Donaldson, 18
    Oberti v. Board of Education of the Borough of Clementon School District, 37
    Pennsylvania Associated for Retarded Children v. Commonwealth of Pennsylvania, 19
    Poolaw v. Parker Unified School District, 37
    Robinson v. California, 17
    Sacramento City Unified School District v. Holland, 37
    Wyatt v. Stickney, 18
    Youngberg v. Romero, 18
  deinstitutionalization, 15, 21–23, 30
  dropout rates, 42, 44–47
  enrollment, 26, 32–33, 42, 44–47, 57, 79, 82, 84, 92, 115
  family, 23
  grants, 29, 133
  incarceration, 16–17, 101, 118, 130
  inclusion, 37
  mainstreaming, 35–37, 134
  politics, 60–61, 117
  population, 33
  public laws
    PL 91-230 (Education of the Handicapped Act), 17–18
    PL 93-112 (Rehabilitation Act of 1973), 26–28
    PL 94-142 (Education for all Handicapped Children Act), 14, 20, 22, 24–28, 39, 66, 103
    PL 95-606 (Amateur Sports Act), 25
    PL 98-199 (Education of the Handicapped Act Amendments of 1983), 25, 28
    PL 99-372 (Handicapped Children's Protection Act), 25, 60
    PL 99-457 (Education of the

Handicapped Act Amendments of 1986), 25
PL 100-360 (Medicare Catastrophic Coverage Act), 26, 28
PL 100-407 (Technology Related Assistance for Individuals with Disabilities Act), 28
PL 101-336 (American with Disabilities Act), 26, 35
PL 101-392 (Carl D. Perkins Vocational and Applied Technology Education Act), 26
PL 101-476 (Individuals with Disabilities Education Act), 14, 21–22, 24–28, 37–39, 58, 66, 88–89, 103
PL 101-496 (Developmental Disabilities Assistance and Bill of Rights Act), 20, 27
PL 101-508 (Child Care and Development Block Grant Act), 27
PL 102-569 (Rehabilitation Act Amendment of 1992), 27
race and ethnicity, 10–11, 30–32, 34–35, 41–46, 53, 124, 135
segregation, 14, 37
services, 18, 20, 24, 33
state mandates, 9–10, 62, 82, 86, 99–100
students, 9, 15, 36, 38, 69. *See also* minorities; special-needs children
studies
  case, 32–33, 75, 115
eleven districts, 9–11, 19, 30–32, 34, 37, 39–47, 53–65, 81–82, 84, 87–89, 91–92, 95–96, 104, 115–16, 119, 134–36
five different schools, 79
substance abuse, 97–98
survival, 89, 113, 118–19
suspension rates, 42, 45, 47
testing and assessment, 10, 20, 24–25, 28, 30–33, 35, 38–39, 45, 56–57, 90–91, 96, 100–101, 103, 118–20, 133–34, 136–37
  Regents exam, 76–77, 116
special-needs children, 66–67, 73, 75, 98, 103. *See also* special education: students
State Tuition Tax Credit and Deduction Program, 106
Success for All program, 38
SURR (schools under registration and review), 92–93, 96

T

Taxpayer Relief Act of 1977, 99
Tech Act. *See* Technology-Related Assistance for Individuals with Disabilities Act
Technology-Related Assistance for Individuals with Disabilities Act, 26, 28
Title I, 57, 59, 101

W

World TEAM Sports, 70